THE CABINET OF CALM

SOOTHING WORDS FOR TROUBLED TIMES

PAUL ANTHONY JONES

Elliott&Thompson

First published 2020 by
Elliott and Thompson Limited
2 John Street
London WC1N 2ES
www.eandtbooks.com

ISBN: 978-1-78396-470-3

9 8 7 6 5 4 3 2 1

A catalogue record for this book is available from the British Library.

Typesetting by Marie Doherty
Printed in the UK by TJ International Ltd

CONTENTS

INTRODUCTION

You probably shouldn't be reading this book. Don't take that the wrong way – truly, I'm very grateful that you are. But here on this opening page, I can't help but feel that it would be nice if we weren't here at all.

There are two reasons why. First of all, this is a book dedicated to words for many of the toughest, most challenging and most worrying times any of us can face. There are chapters here dedicated to unpalatable subjects such as despair and sadness, loss and grief, homesickness and exhaustion. We'll discuss concerns about the state of the world, how fractious and disunited the twenty-first century has proved to be, and how perilously balanced we find the current state of our planet and its environment.

But while the chapters that follow are all dedicated to some troublesome challenge, attached to each is also one of the dictionary's more unusual words or phrases, which, I hope, can give us some much needed aid, reassurance and optimism. The words included here aren't cures as such – the dictionary is an extraordinary thing, but it has yet to come up with a solution for climate change – but rather just some calmative, curative food for thought. These are words to soothe an unquiet mind. To inspire and motivate our creativity. To encourage fellow thinking and community spirit, and to give us fresh hope. In essence, collected here are nothing but kind words, for these unkind times.

It would be nice to think, then, that such a list would not be necessary; if everything were forever right in the world, there would be no demand for this book. Alas, that is not the case. Our world is facing countless challenges, and the times we live in are turbulent and difficult. We each have our own stresses and worries on top of that too – grievances and sadnesses, which every one of us is processing and carrying with us, every moment of every day. Which brings us to the second, and somewhat more personal, reason why this book should perhaps not be in your hands.

In 2018, my dear mam passed away. Then, just eleven weeks later, early in 2019, my dad passed away too. Both of them had been unwell for a long time, but I doubt anyone in our family expected circumstances to play out the way that they did, as swiftly as they did. It was, understandably, an especially cruel and challenging time.

In the aftermath of it all, I determined that I would take some much needed time off. I was tired – more exhausted than I'd ever been in my life – and I needed to recharge my batteries. Maybe I would travel? Finally go and see my good mate out in Australia? After a year of endless hospital appointments and visiting hours, I finally had the time to think about things like that. Just imagine all things I could do with it!

And then, I got an email.

My wonderful publishers – responsible for the book you now hold in your hands – had had an idea.

For almost a decade now, I've written about the oddities and origins of the English language, and in that time have amassed a vast collection of some of its most unusual and remarkable words. How many of these words, my publishers wondered, could be applied to difficult, challenging times – precisely like the ones I had just endured? It was a tantalising idea, unlike anything I'd ever read (or, for that matter, written) before. But, then again – what about my time off? And what about Blake out there in Australia, still waiting for me to go out and visit him after ten years? (Sorry, Blake – it will happen one day . . .) Did I really want to embark on a new project so soon? As it turned out, the answer to that particular question was hanging up in a clothes shop, just a few miles from my home.

A month or so after my dad had passed away, I found myself ambling around the city centre near my home here in Newcastle, stretching my legs, taking my mind off things – and mulling over the idea that my publishers had pitched to me. Almost without thinking, I wandered into a clothes shop on the high street, and there, hanging on one of the rails, was one of my dad's shirts. Not a particularly meaningful one – not a favourite of his, nor some designer name – just a shirt. But seeing it there almost knocked me off my feet.

From nowhere, the events of the previous months came flooding back. It seemed finally to dawn on me that my wonderful parents, after a year of horrors neither of them deserved, had both gone. I would never see or speak or laugh with them ever again. And this shirt – this simple, not particularly meaningful shirt – was the proof of precisely that.

Needless to say, I had to leave the shop.

Oddly, that sudden rush of re-remembered grief vanished almost as quickly as it had arrived, and by the time I was back outside on the high street, I was fine again. The entire episode had lasted perhaps less than thirty seconds. Perplexed by the entire thing, I stopped to buy a coffee, set off walking home, and had just one thought in my mind: *there's a word for that.*

A few years before the Shirt Incident, I stumbled across the word *stound* in an old Scots dialect dictionary I'd bought from a second-hand bookshop in St Andrews. A *stound*, this dictionary told me, was a sudden pang of grief when a loss is unexpectedly remembered. When I had first found this word, it struck me as interesting, so I posted it on Twitter, and pulled together a short blog post about it. But now, several years later – having lived through and now experienced precisely what that word encapsulated – it finally struck me how meaningful and important that humble-looking word actually is. But it also struck me that, somehow, having a word like that in my linguistic armoury, to describe that awful rush of pain and sorrow, felt comforting: it meant that someone, somewhere, at some point in the past had experienced precisely the same thing themselves – to such an extent, in fact, that they felt compelled to invent a word for it. Somehow that made it feel as if I wasn't the only one struggling through this awful time. And for every word like *stound*, I reasoned, there had to be countless others out there that could provide some similar reassurance and solace, and bring a little bit of comfort to the toughest of tough times.

My mind was made up. I needed to write this book.

So now, here it is. The word *stound* is here, of course, alongside fifty more of the English language's most obscure and extraordinary words. And every single one of them is, it's hoped, in some way fit to assuage some of the pain and anguish from some of life's challenges, offer a little inspiration and food for thought, and some soothing reassurance.

Perhaps we'd all still not rather be here – after all, it really would be nice to think that bad things don't happen. But now that we *are* all here, let's see if we can help each other out.

AGANIPPE

≈

for when you're lacking inspiration

'You can't wait for inspiration,' Jack London famously said. 'You have to go after it with a club.' In a sense, he was right. The longer you sit with a blank page or a blank canvas in front of you (even if it's only a metaphorical one), the more likely it is that your thoughts will wander, time tick by, and what little inspiration or motivation you might have had will be soon swallowed up by daydreams and self-doubt. Rather than busy yourself with the work at hand, you end up questioning your ability to do it, questioning *why* you're doing it and questioning how worthwhile it would be even if you *were* to do it at all.

And still, throughout it all, that blank page remains steadfastly there.

It's perhaps for good reason that the word *inspiration*

derives from the same root as words such as *respiration* and *perspiration*: descended from the Latin *spirare*, meaning 'to breathe', etymologically *inspiration* is the 'breath' of life or action, while to be *inspired* is to breathe life into whatever task you have at hand. Suffering a lack of inspiration can consequently feel stifling. Without that animating stimulus to kick-start your work, your thoughts can feel held back, your ideas choked and the task at hand ever more lifeless.

The word *spirit* itself derives from that same life-giving Latin root too – which is somewhat appropriate, given that *inspiration* was originally applied only in religious contexts, to describe acts (and later, works of scripture and theological literature) supposed to have been produced by authors under the direct guidance of God. Unfortunately, it's unlikely that some kind of divine intervention is going to help you finish off that office presentation, fire away that email currently languishing in your drafts, or come up with a crowd-pleasing one-liner for your best man's speech. And if you're waiting for the hand of some almighty power to step in and pen the perfect opening line of that novel you've been promising to write for years, then you might be in for a long wait. Instead, what you need is an *Aganippe*.

An *Aganippe* (pronounced 'ah-gah-NIP-ee', along the same lines as *Mississippi*) is a source of literary, poetic or artistic inspiration. In Greek mythology, it was the name of one of two fountains at the foot of Mount Helicon, the grand mountain in central Greece held sacred by those sister goddesses of art and artistic inspiration, the Nine Muses. Legend has it that the waters of both the Aganippe (whose name combines the Greek words for 'sweet' and 'horse') and its neighbouring stream the Hippocrene (literally the 'horse-fountain') sprang from hoof-prints of the magnificent winged horse Pegasus. Given such impressive origins and surroundings, it was understandable that drinking the fountain's crystalline waters was thought to be a sure-fire method of reinvigorating one's poetic and artistic inspiration.

It would be nice to think that nothing more than a refreshing mouthful of cool spring water could magically cure a creative logjam, but in truth there is no quick fix. With no magical stream to sup from, writers in the fifteenth and sixteenth centuries instead raided the Greek myths themselves for their inspiration, adopting the words *Aganippe* and *Hippocrene* (and even *muse* itself) as bywords for whatever or whoever inspired their work. And it's that approach that can be useful to us today.

No matter the task at hand, when stimulus or motivation are in short supply, consider the *Aganippe* as a
reminder that it always helps to turn to something that
inspires you to help see your project through – no matter what shape or form that inspiration might take.
It could be a favourite book, work of art or piece of
music. It could even be a cherished place or walk – a
much needed break in the open air to clear the mind
and reboot your ideas. Or perhaps it will prove to be
an energising, idea-bouncing conversation with a good
friend or mentor.

Then again, perhaps the problem is less a lack of
inspiration, and more an absence of motivation? In
which case, your personal *Aganippe* might be the reward
you promise yourself for when the task you're currently
struggling to finish (or start) is finally complete. After
all, if you're stuck in a lethargic rut, sometimes nothing
more than the sense of relief or achievement you will
feel when you finally chalk some longstanding task off
your to-do list is enough to get those creative gears back
in motion.

See also: autoschediasm, mooreeffoc, psaphonise

AGATHISM

≋

for when you're feeling disillusionment
or struggling to remain positive

It can be difficult to stay optimistic when times are hard. Even the brightest and most upbeat of outlooks on life can be turned on its head by some unwelcome shift in circumstances or a run of tough luck. When those hard times seem to be all around us – personally, locally, nationally and even globally – then the weight of all those troubles and problems can prove even more difficult to escape. Your customary optimism drifts slowly towards pessimism and, as dark clouds gather on the horizon, it proves all too easy to sink into gloomy disillusionment.

Thankfully, there is a superb word worth holding on to at times like these (albeit a fairly obscure and unfamiliar one). To appreciate both it and the role it

takes in our vocabulary fully, we first need to understand
a pair of much more familiar words, whose meanings
and origins are perhaps a little more complex than we
might appreciate.

Today, we think of *optimism* as little more than a syn-
onym for positivity or hopefulness, but that hasn't always
been the case. Derived from *optimum*, Latin for 'best',
its roots lie in the philosophical writings of Gottfried
Leibniz, an eighteenth-century German mathemat-
ician, thinker and inventor whose work across countless
fields formed one of the cornerstones of the European
Enlightenment.

In 1710, Leibniz published a collection of essays on
'the Goodness of God, the Freedom of Man and the
Origin of Evil', called the *Théodicée*. In it, he introduced
the theory that this world – our world – must surely
be the greatest of all possible worlds. 'As it is in mathematics when there is no maximum nor minimum',
he wrote, 'everything is done equally – or, when that
is not possible, nothing is done at all. So may it be said
likewise . . . that if this were not the best [*or*] optimum
among all possible worlds, God would not have produced any at all.'

In other words, Leibniz believed that any divine
creator we wish to credit with the existence of our

world must, we can presume, have been happy with their creation. If they were not, surely they would have been omnipotent enough, and felt compelled enough, to abandon this world and start again, improving on any mistakes or shortcomings in their grand redesign. Ultimately, the fact that this world and everything in it exists and continues to exist at all – regardless of its flaws and problems – proves without question that it is the best world that any great creative force could ever possibly have wrought.

Later writers and philosophers picked up on Leibniz's theory and expanded on it, with his fellow Enlightenment thinker Voltaire first attaching the word *optimism* to it in 1737. So far from meaning simply 'positivity' or 'hopefulness', *optimism* referred originally to Leibniz's grand notion that our world is the best of all possible worlds, where the most good can be achieved with the least amount of evil.

Whereas *optimism* derives from the Latin for 'best', its opposite, *pessimism*, came to us from the Latin for 'worst', *pessimus*. It first emerged somewhat later than its positive counterpart, in the late eighteenth century, as a general term for the worst or most deprived possible condition of something. As Leibniz's theory became more widespread, however, *pessimism* came to be attached to a model or viewpoint entirely antithetical to it – namely, that this world is the worst of all possible worlds, as its innumerable flaws, inequities and imperfections bear out.

From these philosophical beginnings, it wasn't until the nineteenth century that the meanings of *optimism* and *pessimism* finally began to broaden, and they began to be used, as they still are today, to refer merely to hopefulness and hopelessness, and positivity and negativity, respectively. Back when they still represented these two polar opposite theories – these profound and strictly defined outlooks on life – a third term was coined to occupy the middle ground between them. Between the two extremes of *optimism* and *pessimism* lies *agathism* – a word that is well worth holding on to when times turn hard and it becomes difficult to see a tolerable future.

In 1816, Dr George Miller, a fellow of the Royal Irish Academy, gave an address in which he spoke of a colleague at the University of Dublin who considered himself 'not an optimist, but an agathist'. His colleague, Miller continued, 'did not think himself competent to determine what was absolutely the best', but despite the obvious problems and flaws in the world today, nevertheless believed that 'everything tended to good'. It was Dr Miller's speech that seemingly first sparked interest in the term *agathism*, and from there the word fell into occasional use in nineteenth-century philosophical discussions as the implications of Dr Miller's address – and his colleague's personal outlook on life – began to be considered more widely.

Agathism is ultimately defined as the doctrine that all things tend eventually to work towards the good, but the means of getting there – and of deciding precisely what constitutes good and bad – might not be easy. It is possible, the so-called *agathist* believes, for this world to be on an ever improving trajectory while still suffering flaws and setbacks, troubles and countless imperfections. Indeed, sometimes these flaws and setbacks are necessary in order to learn from our mistakes and build and prepare for a fairer, better and more robust world in the future. *Agathism* stands as a more level-headed alternative to *optimism* and *pessimism*; elements of both viewpoints are accepted, but the world is not seen so extremely as the 'best' or 'worst' of anything. For that reason, etymologically, *agathism* simply derives from *agathos*, the Greek word for 'good'.

No matter which of these theories seems to strike a chord with you, *agathism* can be a timely reminder that, although things might not be quite so bright right now, they will be brighter in the future. All we have to do is

wait, enduring the bad times as best we can, and focusing on the good times that will – no matter how distant
they might feel at the moment – eventually return.

See also: eucatastrophe, interfulgent, meliorism

ALLABORATE

≋

for when you're disappointed with progress

It's not a particularly comforting thought, but disappointment really is a fact of life. Best intentions and ideas can be all too easily thwarted and dashed – often by little more than a simple change of circumstance or fortune that no amount of preparation could have prevented.

It might be a familiar feeling, but disappointment can nevertheless sometimes prove a difficult emotion to navigate, not least because it so often follows a lengthy period of exhaustive preparation, or nervous, adrenaline-raising anticipation. How much more crushing does a disappointment feel when we've allowed ourselves to daydream beforehand about how wonderful the future could be, only to have it fail to come to pass, or fall far short of our heightened expectations? One word for this is *anticipointment*, widely claimed as having been coined in a 1960s American ad campaign for greetings cards.

As for our all-too-tempting propensity to indulge in unrealistic daydreams, destined only to end in disappointment, there's a word for that too – and attached to it is a wonderful tale of ruinous pride and thoughtless ambition: *Alnascharism*.

Alnaschar, according to *The Story of the Barber's Sixth Brother* in the *Arabian Nights* anthology, was a tradesman in ancient Baghdad. Having inherited a modest sum of money from his father, Alnaschar decided to invest it all in a basket of glassware, which he intended to sell for a grand profit from his stall in the local marketplace. As he sat waiting for his first customer, however, he allowed his mind to wander, and he began to indulge himself in imagining how his ambitious money-making scheme would ultimately – and undoubtedly – triumph.

By continually reinvesting all of his profits in ever more valuable merchandise, he would keep doubling his investment and eventually become wealthy enough to live in a grand palace. Once there, he would win the heart of the local vizier's beautiful young daughter. As his thoughts grew ever more wild and unrealistic, Alnaschar began to picture himself as a magnificent and imperious power-crazed tycoon, formidable enough to treat everyone around him with disdain and contempt. Now entirely lost in his daydreams, he finally envisaged an angry confrontation with the vizier and his beautiful new bride, and, in his imagined rage, lashed out wildly – only to snap out of his daydream to find that he had kicked over his basket of glassware and smashed it all to pieces on the stony ground. In the end, he was left with nothing – aside from his unfulfilled dream. It is from this tale that we have adopted the word *Alnascharism*: coined in the eighteenth century to refer to the act of indulging in hopeless fantasies, destined only to lead to fruitless and disastrous disappointment.

Not that all our disappointments need lead to utter *Alnascharistic* ruin. Many day-to-day disappointments are slight and inconsequential, mere nuisances or inconveniences that are soon dealt with and forgotten. But some are more hurtful, and the stings in their discomforting tails can smart for a considerable time afterwards. Of these, few disappointments are as demoralising as seeing an absence of progress, despite our staunchest and most exhaustive efforts.

We don't need to be as wildly ambitious as Alnaschar to set our sights on some new goal in our lives, whether it be something as trivial as dropping a few pounds or getting into shape ahead of a holiday, or some longer-term project, such as learning a new language or studying a musical instrument. After the first flush of enthusiasm, it can be disheartening not to see our efforts pay off as quickly as we might like. Before long, we can easily fall back into old habits, and eventually shelve our ambitions altogether.

Toiling arduously but seeing little reward for your efforts is called *pingling* according to the *English Dialect Dictionary* (1898), while to *wurdle*, according to the *Scottish National Dictionary*, is 'to work hard with little prospect of success'. While we're busy advancing the vocabulary of disappointment, there is, I'm glad to say, a more positive word worth bearing in mind: to *allaborate* something is to improve it steadily and painstakingly over time.

In the sense of advancing or expanding on something, *allaborate* is an etymological cousin of *elaborate*, and both words share the same Latin root as the likes of *labour* and *laborious*. But while *elaborate* gained the connotation of making something more intricate or impressive, *allaborate* came simply to mean 'to work hard on something' – and thereby, with time, gradually to improve it.

It is a word well worth bearing in mind when you're feeling as though your efforts in some new endeavour are not paying off, or when your progress seems slow to non-existent. It is a word to remind us that change and advancement never happen overnight, but one day, one lesson, one workout or one informed choice at a time. And it is a reminder to stay focused on your goal, no matter how remote or unobtainable it might seem.

See also: psaphonise

ANACAMPSEROTE

≋

for when you're in a struggling relationship

Even the strongest and most enduring of relationships can come under pressure from time to time. Often these bumps in the road are nothing more than that: short-lived, swiftly forgotten quarrels and wrangles that, while upsetting at the time, quickly heal, and can even lead to stronger bonds in the future. At other times, however, these rough patches can prove more difficult to negotiate.

A relationship that is coming to its natural conclusion is different from one that is merely negotiating one of these momentary glitches and working to find its way back on track – and it's not always easy to tell the difference. Should you find yourself at the unhappy end of a once happy relationship, you can turn to the entry for DRUERY for some comforting words. But for a faltering relationship or a dimmed romance that merely needs rekindling, there is another word that offers some welcome solace and advice.

Anacampserote is the name of a fabled plant, once supposed by folklorists and herbalists to have the ability to repair a failing or extinguished romance. 'A certain herb', as one seventeenth-century dictionary defined it, 'whose touch reneweth decayed love.'

The beautiful name *anacampserote* pulls together three separate Greek roots: *ana*, meaning 'back' or 'again' (as in *anagram*); *kampe*, a Greek word meaning 'bend' or 'curve' (which might be a distant relative of *campus*, and, oddly, thanks to their shape, is the etymological ancestor of the humble *scampi*), and *eros*, a Greek word for love (which is unsurprisingly the origin of words including *erotic* and *erogenous*). Put together, those three elements give us a handsome word that could effectively be interpreted as 'a love turned back on itself' – or, as is perhaps more the case here, 'a love returned once more'.

As striking as this word is, it remains something of a linguistic rarity, seldom encountered outside dictionaries and textbooks since the early 1600s. So rare is *anacampserote*, in fact, that we actually know very little of any substance about it: were it ever a genuine plant at all, we have no clue as to what it was, nor what it looked like, and seemingly nor has anyone ever felt the need to record the means by which disconsolate lovers were meant to obtain it, prepare it or otherwise ensure its effectiveness in rekindling romance. So if you were hoping to track down a sprig of this herbalist's charm to relight the spark in your own romance, there's little hard information to go on. Instead, perhaps we're better off interpreting this word not literally, but figuratively. In order to rekindle a dwindling romance, we really need to find a metaphorical *anacampserote*.

Perhaps you and your partner's own *anacampserote* is the bright memory of a favourite restaurant, a favourite film or a favourite place. Perhaps it's nothing more than a song, a photograph, a joke or a fondly remembered anecdote that instantly takes you back to happier times. We don't need to rely on legendary botanical cure-alls to 'renew a decayed love', as that ancient dictionary put it, but merely remember what sparked that romantic connection in the first place. Anything that serves to remind you of why you are both still together is surely more effective than any age-old folkloric remedy.

See also: druery, redamancy

ANGEL-VISITS

≈

for when you're missing your friends

While *cupboard love* is feigned affection, expressed only by someone who stands to gain from it, a *cupboard friend* is an insincere companion, whose dissembling acts of friendship are intended to benefit only themselves. The earliest record of *cupboard love* dates from the 1700s, while the duplicitous, self-serving *cupboard friend* first appeared in the title of a nineteenth-century poem, bemoaning the impolite behaviour of an unwanted dining companion:

> Frank carves very ill, yet will palm all the meat;
> He eats more than six, and drinks more than he eats.
> Four pipes, after dinner, he constantly smokes
> And seasons his wit with impertinent jokes.
> Yet sighing, he says, we must certainly break;

And my cruel unkindness compels him to speak,
For of late I invite him – but four times a week.

The British Martial; Or an Anthology
of English Epigrams (1806)

While the nineteenth century gave us the mooch-
ing *cupboard friend*, it also gave us a word for its direct
opposite. According to the *English Dialect Dictionary*, a
bread-and-cheese friend is 'a true friend, as distinguished
from a cupboard lover', someone who can be relied on
in all circumstances.

Quite what the reference to 'bread and cheese' is
meant to signify here is debatable, though perhaps it
alludes to a companion so faithful and reliable that they
remain loyal even in hard times, when only the most
meagre of offerings is on the table. The *bread-and-cheese
friend* is just one noteworthy entry in the dictionary's
long vocabulary of friendship.

A *jolly-dog*, for instance, is a boon companion – a
friend who can always be relied on for a riotously good
time. In sixteenth-century English, your best friend was
your *cockmate*, or your *shop-fellow*, while in some southern
dialects they were apparently (and somewhat confus-
ingly) once known as your *Dutch cousin*. An undyingly
loyal friend is an *Achates* (pronounced 'ah-KAY-teez'), an

allusion to a tireless companion of Aeneas, the legendary hero of the Latin epic poem the *Aeneid*.

A *jamb-friend* is someone with whom you can effortlessly talk the night away; referring to one of the upright timbers or *jambs* that forms the margin of a hearth, it literally describes someone with whom you would happily relax at a fireside. Likewise, while an *inkleweaver* in eighteenth-century English was someone who sewed by the light and warmth of a fireplace, proverbially *to be as thick as inkleweavers* is to be inseparably good friends.

The kindness, company and counsel of a good friend could solve most of the problems identified in this book. After all, when times are hard, turning to someone you trust and admire, and with whom you have countless shared memories, is all but guaranteed to make you feel better. But if your friends are not around to help – what then?

A word worth bearing in mind for times such as these is *angel-visits* – visits or catch-ups with good friends that prove all too few and far between. It might seem cruel if you are missing your friends to emphasise a word that draws attention to the fact that you see them so infrequently, but there is more to this word than that.

Hidden behind the simple dictionary definition of *angel-visits* are all the memories you and your best friends share, which together act as a reminder of why you are such great companions, and why you so look forward to seeing them again. Don't use this word to focus on the pain of not having your friends close at hand, but to cheer yourself with your shared memories, and to look forward to whenever you will next see one another, to remind yourself of how important they are to you, and how lucky you are to know them.

The term *angel-visit* alludes to the apparent infrequency of actual heavenly visitations. It was in the early 1700s that it first came to be used to refer to equally infrequent reunions with good friends and family. This poem neatly encapsulates the feeling of how comforting, though regretfully sporadic, these visits and catch-ups can be:

> How fading are the joys we dote upon!
> Like apparitions seen and gone:
> But those which soonest take their flight,
> Are the most exquisite and strong;
> Like angels' visits, short and bright;
> Mortality's too weak to bear them long.
>
> John Norris, 'The Parting' (*c.*1700)

See also: antipelargy, heafgang, howffy, minding

ANTIPELARGY

≈

for when you're missing your family

Parents who are not yet willing to tell their children all the details about where babies come from have been relying on euphemistic tales of storks depositing new-born infants down household chimneys since the mid nineteenth century. It's a curious story, supposedly arising from nothing more than the tendency of storks, cranes and other long-legged birds to nest on rooftops and chimneystacks. But even more curiously, this titbit of folklore isn't the stork's only connection with our family life.

One of the dictionary's more inventive etymological stories is that found behind the word *pedigree*, which can be traced back more than seven centuries to a French phrase, *pied de gru*, literally meaning a 'stork's' or 'crane's foot'. Supposedly, the broad sibling-spanning horizontal lines that connect the family members on genealogical diagrams so reminded medieval scribes of storks' feet that they adopted the phrase for these ancestral networks. Centuries of use and misuse then transformed that original French phrase into the word we use today, and as *pied de gru* morphed into *pedigree*, the stork's connection to our family trees was lost to an etymological footnote.

Lurking among the less familiar words in the dictionary is another term we owe to the stork. The Greek name for the stork was *pelargos*, which linguistic folklore would have you believe brings together two Greek roots meaning 'dark', *pelos*, and 'white', *argos*, in reference to the bird's striking monochrome plumage. In antiquity, storks enjoyed a reputation for being among the bird world's most diligently attentive and affectionate parents, with various tales from Greek and Roman legend claiming that young storks repaid their parents' kindnesses by supporting their weight in flight in their old age, and that, at the end of their lives, storks were rewarded for their dutiful parental skills by being transformed into humans and permitted to raise human children. All of this lore is neatly captured in *antipelargy*, a criminally underused word for the reciprocal, automatic and unquestioning love that connects parents to their children, and vice versa. 'A mutual thankfulness or requital of a benefit,' as one dictionary from the early eighteenth century grandly put it, especially – in light of the storks' care for their elders – that of 'a child's nourishing a parent in old age'.

Antipelargy might seem an odd word to focus on in an entry dedicated to the feeling of missing one's family. The security, warmth and feeling of belonging that constitute *antipelargy* can leave an agonising gulf when it is lost or far removed. If you are far away from home or your nearest and dearest are now no longer just a few short streets or a telephone call away, this might seem like an especially painful word. But in times when we feel we are missing that warmth and familial companionship, it is worth bearing in mind that those *antipelargic* bonds are extraordinarily strong, and do not simply disintegrate or disappear when those whom it connects are far removed from one another. Certainly, there are times when this closeness might not always feel as if it is within immediate reach, but that is not to say that it is not there at all. *Antipelargy* is stronger and more enduring than all the air miles and motorways fragmenting our modern lives.

See also: angel-visits, howffy, minding

APHERCOTROPISM

≋

for when you're facing obstacles

Everything is going swimmingly, and then – well, not so much. Life throws a stumbling block into your path and suddenly you and everything else that was heading down the clear open road in front of you is forced to grind to a halt.

Few things are more frustrating than being held back by circumstances out of your control, no matter whether they are just trivial annoyances and nuisances that can be rapidly fixed or surmounted, or larger problems that may take days or weeks – if not even longer – to overcome. So, if everything has gone awry, and suddenly you find an unexpected obstacle in your way, what word can best motivate you to face up to the problem ahead, and begin to work around it? Oddly, the answer to that question might lie in your back garden.

Aphercotropism is the name of the phenomenon that accounts for plants and trees gradually extending their shoots, stems, roots and leaves around any obstacles they encounter, manoeuvring their way through the gaps between fence posts and iron railings, and the fashioning of the intricate geometric labyrinths by the roots of urban trees, as they find their way through the cracks and fissures between paving stones. It differs from processes such as *phototropism* (a plant's movement towards a light source) and *hydrotropism* (a movement towards water), in that with *aphercotropism* the plant's movement is not dictated by something that it requires, like water or sunlight, but by something that is impeding it, which it must bypass in order to continue developing. For that reason, *aphercotropism* – derived from Greek roots meaning 'wall' or 'barrier' (*herkos*) and 'growth' (*tropos*) – literally means 'turning away from an obstruction'.

This phenomenon was first described by Charles Darwin, who outlined a simple but effective experiment he had carried out on pea shoots in his 1880 work *The Power of Movement in Plants*. Darwin found that by gluing a small piece of card to the tip of a shoot, the plant would steadily divert its normal upward growth off to one side, working its way around the edge of the card before resuming its ordinary vertical growth. Nothing, it seemed, would stop the plant from doing precisely what it needed to survive.

He might have discovered this phenomenon, but Darwin didn't name it; the term *aphercotropism* itself did not appear in print until almost two decades after his original study, when this experiment was recounted in an 1899 edition of *Nature Notes*, the journal of an early conservationist organisation called the Selborne Society. Precisely who coined the term in the nineteen years in between is a mystery.

When something stops us in our path, it is often all too tempting to give up, or give in. Perhaps, we reason, whatever endeavour we're currently embarked on simply isn't worth the extra effort. Or perhaps this latest set-back, hindering our progress, might feel like one setback too many. In such times, there is a lesson to be learned from *aphercotropism*.

What that word reminds us – and, for that matter, what Darwin's simple experiment with the pea shoot tells us – is that there is *always* a way around our problems and obstacles. It might take time, and it might take effort (perhaps considerably more effort than we previously thought), but there will nevertheless be a solution. What frustrates us at this moment might seem insurmountable, but if a humble pea shoot can quietly and diligently change its course of action, and calmly work its way around the obstacle currently in its path, then surely we can too. There will always be light at the end of the tunnel – or, perhaps more appropriately, on the other side of the card.

See also: traumatropism

ARMOGAN

≋

for when you've missed an opportunity

It is an odd twist of our language that when it crops up, the word *opportunity* is all too often spun into a negative context, and handed connotations tinged with loss, regret or hurt. Proverbially we are told that *opportunity knocks* – but we're also told that it *never knocks twice*. Acting *opportunistically* is often taken to imply a certain underhandedness, or a lack of principles. Economists talk of the *opportunity cost* of making a choice or decision, selecting just one option from a series of choices, and thereby rendering all its alternatives null and void. *Man's extremity is God's opportunity*, warns another ancient proverb, pointing out that we often turn to a higher power for help or guidance only in times of difficulty. And we are warned too that, given half a chance, *opportunity maketh the thief.*

In the murkier corners of the dictionary we find a whole vocabulary to do with missed, lost or regretted opportunities. *Latter-wit* and *afterlight* are both words for knowledge or realisations that come too late to be of use. *Noforsooth* is an impossibly rare seventeenth-century verb meaning 'to squander an opportunity by turning down a suitor'. And a *corbie-messenger* is a messenger who arrives too late to be of use – an allusion to the raven or 'corbie' that was first released by Noah from the Ark, never to return.

Opportunity itself, however, is an inherently positive word. Derived from the same Latin root as *port*, it literally means 'towards a harbour', and is thought to have been used originally to describe winds or currents that could be relied on (or else, happened entirely by chance) to direct and carry a vessel safely back to the shore. Our language's obsession with putting a negative spin on the *opportunities* we encounter, clearly, is one we have fostered ourselves.

It is easy to see where such negativity might come from. Missed, lost or unfairly stolen opportunities can sting, and it is all too easy to become obsessed with what might have been if only we had acted differently, more swiftly or more perceptively. What we need, then, is a word to restore our faith in opportunity – to reassure us that all need not be lost when a chance appears to pass us by. And that no matter what we may regret missing out on, there might well be better chances and opportunities in the future.

That word is *armogan*. Like *opportunity* before it, *armogan* is a word with distant nautical origins, and was likewise defined by one nineteenth-century dictionary as merely a word for a 'favourable wind'. Its meaning, however, appears to have been more specific: according to another Victorian-era guide to maritime jargon, *armogan* was 'a Mediterranean word for fine weather', used as 'an old term for good opportunity, or season for navigation'. Put another way, *armogan* describes the optimal weather conditions for embarking on a new journey.

Aside from being merely a long-forgotten naval term, the etymology of *armogan* is unclear. A tantalising clue is provided by the fact that, in 1876, it was listed in a naval *Glossary of Anglo-Norman and Gascon Words*, which, rather than merely writing it off as 'a Mediterranean word', would suggest that its roots lie specifically in southwest France. If that's the case, then it's likely *armogan* is descended from some choice word from the Occitan language – and indeed folk etymology would have you believe it derives from an Occitan word for 'apricot', *armonhan*, perhaps in reference to the warming apricot-orange colour of a calm coastal sunrise. That theory is still only conjecture, however, and with a dearth of written evidence to go on, it seems likely the word will remain something of an etymological puzzle. But what concerns us more here is that *armogan* is a word relating to optimal timing.

Back in the days when it apparently first appeared in the language, setting out on a journey as potentially perilous as a voyage on the open sea would have been entirely dependent on the weather conditions in and around port. If those conditions are not perfectly suitable – or, rather, not *armogan* – then the entire journey would simply have to be postponed or abandoned altogether. In that sense, this is a word to remind us that holding back on taking action is not always a sign of a missed opportunity, but a sign that the time is not yet right. Moreover, not acting when we have the chance by no means implies that the same opportunity – or perhaps an even more favourable one – might still come to pass.

Much as we might kick ourselves for not acting when we had the opportunity, and much as we might have a tendency to hold on to our regrets and missed chances, sometimes the extra time we give ourselves by holding back gives us a chance to learn from our actions (or inactions) and better prepare for future opportunities

as and when they arise. Just like the crew of a ship waiting for a storm to clear to begin their next adventure,
the word *armogan* reminds us that though we might have
missed one opportunity, another even better one might
be just around the corner.

See also: kengood

AUTOSCHEDIASM

≈

for when you're stuck in a rut

In 1879, a French naturalist named Jean-Henri Fabre was observing a wasp in the garden of his home in Sérignan-du-Comtat, near Avignon in the south of France, when he happened to spot something unusual in its behaviour. The wasp in question was a digger wasp, one of a vast family of insects with the scientific name *Sphex*, the Greek word for 'wasp', which lays its eggs in holes and indentations made in the soil. Fabre knew that to ensure their subterranean offspring have a guaranteed first meal ready for immediately after they hatch, *Sphex* wasps employ an ingenious if somewhat grisly ploy: using their stings, they paralyse some unlucky prey animal, typically a cricket or caterpillar, and haul it below ground before depositing a single egg beside it. They then seal the entrance to the chamber and depart to find

another suitable nest spot – leaving the hapless caterpillar, often still alive but now utterly immobile, to act as a
living food store for the developing larva. Fabre wanted
to witness this grim display for himself – but the wasp
he was observing proved herself to be an extra-diligent
mother.

Having caught a caterpillar and hauled it over to the
entrance to her nest hole, the mother wasp paused for
a moment, Fabre observed, before depositing the caterpillar on the ground while she crawled inside alone,
ostensibly to ensure that all was still well. No matter
the number of nest sites he followed the wasp to – and
no matter the type of prey or the number of eggs she
laid – the mother *Sphex* wasp's behaviour remained the
same at every one: she always carried out this final sur-
vey before she was seemingly satisfied enough to lay her
precious egg.

To test the mother's diligence, Fabre decided to play
a trick on her. While she was below ground once again
double-checking that her latest nest site was suitable, he
moved the caterpillar she had left on the surface away
from the entrance, simulating it having been caught
by the wind and blown astray while it was out of her
sight. When she returned to the surface, Fabre found
she promptly relocated her prey, picked it back up in her

jaws and carried it back over to the entrance to her hole, entirely unfazed. But then, rather than her continuing straight back into the chamber as expected, Fabre saw that she yet again paused, deposited the caterpillar on the ground, and repeated precisely the same underground inspection that she had carried out just moments earlier. Moreover, Fabre found that no matter how many times he repeated this test – removing the caterpillar from the chamber entrance while the mother was out of sight – she always stopped to carry out the same preliminary checks, every single time.

Fabre's curious discovery of the seemingly robotically instinctive behaviour of nesting digger wasps languished in dusty animal behaviour textbooks and natural history journals for the following century, serving as little more than an interesting aside or anecdote passed from one naturalist to another. But, in 1982, it suddenly found a new and unexpected audience when the American cognitive scientist Douglas Hofstadter included a retelling of Fabre's *Sphex* story in an essay on mechanical, unconscious behaviour in humans. And in doing so, he coined a fantastic word to describe precisely that:

> This is a rather shocking revelation of the mech-
> anical underpinning, in a living creature, of what

looks like quite reflective behaviour. There seems
to be something supremely unconscious about the
wasp's behaviour here, something totally opposite
to what we feel we are all about, particularly when
we talk about our own consciousness. I propose to
call the quality here portrayed sphexishness, and its
opposite antisphexishness.

'On the Seeming Paradox of Mechanizing
Creativity', *Scientific American* (1982)

Later writers and theorists have since elaborated on
Hofstadter's notion of *sphexishness*, applying it more specifically to behaviour that appears on the surface to be
conscious, intelligent or informed, but on closer inspection proves merely mechanical – even to the extent of
seeming to go against our better thoughts or instincts.
In that sense, Hofstadter coined a supremely useful term
for mindless, robotic, stuck-in-a-rut toil or behaviour
(as well as its opposite, *antisphexishness*, which he quite
rightly described as 'a vexish word to pronounce').

Admittedly, there can't be many words worth knowing that derive from the breeding behaviour of wasps,
but *sphexishness* proves there is at least one. It is a word
to describe grim, mind-numbing repetitiveness – the
dreariness of an everyday routine that has become so

deeply ingrained that you can drift through it mindlessly, with little thought to what's actually going on around you. It is a word for the monotony of a daily commute, the tiresomeness of an unchallenging job and the tedium of an unchanging schedule. Wake at the same time each day to catch the same bus or train, or to commute down the same roads with the same sights and sounds, to arrive at the same places, day after day, and before long everything begins to drift into one long exercise in *sphexish* behaviour.

If we have a word for the problem here, what word can we rely on to address it?

For a tired commuter or city worker bored with mindlessly journeying down the same cramped streets each day, an interesting word to indicate a possible escape from this monotony is *psychogeography*. Coined in 1955, *psychogeography* was originally the name of an avant-garde artistic and architectural technique intended to spark debate about how the manmade world around us influences our nature and thinking. Advocates of this technique took inspiration from the idle, people-watching wanderers or *flâneurs* of the nineteenth century, who would stroll the towns and cities of Europe with no particular plan or destination in mind, and merely observe the comings and goings of the people who lived

there. The *psychogeographers* of the 1950s and 1960s likewise based their work on random wanderings through
urban environments, seeking out new and intriguing
features of the architecture of their towns and cities, and
reflecting on how the different urban spaces they came
across affected how they felt and acted.

As this technique became more widely known, use
of the word *psychogeography* broadened. While the art
movement had been based on randomly wandering the
streets of towns and cities, *psychogeography* came to be
applied to any act of leisurely meandering around familiar areas, with no set destination in mind, seeking out
new and interesting places. It is, ultimately, a means of
seeing the everyday world around us through new eyes,
and thereby finding a new appreciation for what it has
to offer. (Flick ahead to MOOREEFFOC for more on that.)

The monotony of *sphexishness* is not unique to the
city-dwelling commuter. The dreariness of a routine
can affect anyone, from the frazzled parent, fitting in the
same errands and after-school classes around the same
school bells each day, to the leisurely retiree, who, now
with no work-based schedule to fit around, nevertheless
falls into a set pattern of the same places, faces, chores
and activities week after week. The problem here is not
what makes our lives routine, but the fact that they can

so easily *become* routine. We need a solution that inspires us to break that monotony, no matter what its root cause might be. We need an *autoschediasm*.

An *autoschediasm* is something done spontaneously, entirely on the spur of the moment, or without any prior preparation. The word was coined in the 1800s, but its earlier derivatives (notably the adjective *autoschediastical*) have been knocking around the fringes of the English language since the seventeenth century, and its roots lie in an Ancient Greek word, *autoschedios*, used to describe an offhand remark or action, or an unprepared, impromptu address, more than two millennia ago.

After *sphexishness* and *psychogeography*, admittedly *autoschediasm* is another clumsy mouthful of a word, but no matter – it is what it represents that concerns us here. *Autoschediasm* is a timely reminder that, in a world of mundane routine and robotic monotony, giving in to spontaneity every once in a while can prove energising and inspiring. After all, our lives are only routine if we *allow* them to become routine, and seeking out a few chances and opportunities outside of our everyday world is a simple and effective way of breaking that routine apart. These *autoschediasms* don't need to be world-changing either – no need (at least, as yet) to drop everything and go off travelling the world. A break from routine can be sparked by the smallest of changes to our day-to-day lives. Perhaps save that around the world trip for next year . . .

See also: aganippe, mooreeffoc

BEAUTÉ DU DIABLE

≋

for when you're worried about losing your looks

Our appearance changes as we age: our hair turns grey, the lines in our skin deepen and wrinkles begin to develop where once there was clear, smooth skin. For many of us, this is no big deal – nothing more than a simple fact of life. But to others, seeing these changes in appearance can be a difficult and painful realisation. To make matters worse, these concerns are often dismissed as vanity. Sometimes, however, there is more to these worries than there might seem.

As we age, we can do our best to ignore our aches and pains, and laugh off the occasional 'senior moment' of forgetfulness. But ageing becomes a much more tangible and unavoidable process when we see the changes it entails physically – in our bodies, in our faces and right there in our reflection. Looking in the mirror and seeing a visibly older face staring back can be a tangible demonstration that time has passed us by.

Accepting the physical side of the ageing process need not be a challenge, and happily the dictionary offers not one but two words to help us acknowledge it.

The first of these is *antious*, a rare and long-forgotten adjective used simply to describe anything that has become beautiful – or, indeed, more beautiful – purely *because* it has aged. A nineteenth-century dialect invention, the origins of *antious* (as with a lot of dialect terminology) are difficult to pin down, but it is likely just some local corruption of *ancient* or *antique*, reimagined as an inherently and exclusively positive word. Indeed, in its explanation of the term the *English Dialect Dictionary* emphasises that the word *antious* was only ever used of people and things that had grown better or more beautiful with age. Beauty, the dictionary explains, 'is always associated with [the concept of] "old" or "ancient"' when the word *antious* is employed, adding moreover that it is 'difficult to know which of the two is uppermost in the mind of the speaker'. The *English Dialect Dictionary* adds that 'the word is never used when mere age is considered'.

Beauté du diable, meanwhile, is an expression borrowed into English from French in the early nineteenth century. Literally meaning 'the devil's beauty', *beauté du diable* is essentially the opposite of the beauty described in the word *antious*: that is to say, it describes the superficial and often temporary beauty associated with the first flush of youth. Inspired by an old French proverb, *le diable était beau quand il était jeune* ('the Devil was beautiful when he was young'), *beauté du diable* is often more cuttingly applied to beauty that is not only transient, but entirely reliant on youth. 'A nameless charm', as one nineteenth-century definition put it, 'independent of actual beauty'.

What can we take from these two words? Well, *antious* is a reminder that ageing is not only something that comes to everyone and everything, but that what we might think of as a loss of our looks or beauty is merely the acquisition of a different, more mature kind of beauty, unique to all those who have aged. *Beauté du diable*, meanwhile, reminds us that while it might be tempting to be envious of the first flush of youthful beauty, such beauty is often short-lived, skin-deep and depends solely on youthfulness itself.

See also: opsimathy, worldcraft

CARPE NOCTEM

≈

for when you feel you're running out of time

As well as meaning simply an autumnal quality or an 'autumnness' – like that felt in crisp weather or seen in a reddening landscape – the handsome word *autumnity* also has a more figurative and imaginative side. Since the mid 1800s, writers have occasionally employed it as a metaphor for a person's middle age, or the moment or period in a person's life when they realise (or else are compelled to admit to themselves) that they are no longer young. It is essentially a term for a midlife crisis without the crisis: no spontaneous purchasing of a sports car and a leather jacket – merely the quiet and inevitable realisation that one has, as we all do, grown old.

The age at which that realisation takes hold depends on the individual. From leaving school to retiring, life is full of landmarks that serve subtly to remind us of increasing age, and to which we respond in different ways. Some of us accept these landmarks placidly, with grace and pause for thought. After all, ageing is something that comes to us all, and the more philosophical among us might find solace in the realisation that not all of us are lucky enough to see a great many years pass by. To others, however, these milestones come more sharply, and our graceful, slow-dawning *autumnity* becomes less of a quiet stepping stone between one chapter and the next, and more of an alarm bell, a brash wake-up call or the ever louder ticking of a biological clock.

There are a number of words that could be pertinent and reassuring at times like this: the pessimism-defying EUCATASTROPHE or the age-flouting OPSIMATH, for example. But *autumnity* is more than a concern about ageing. After all, the feeling that time is against us – or, for that matter, behind us – and that we have not made the most of the time already gone by can strike at any of life's milestones, not merely those unique to older age.

One familiar motto worth recalling at times like these is *carpe diem*. Its welcome reminder that we should literally 'seize the day' – and in doing so make the most of the present time – is as well known to most people as its origins in the poems of the Roman writer Horace are not. But just as unfamiliar to many people is the nocturnal opposite of *carpe diem*: *carpe noctem*, the injunction to 'seize the night'.

Alas we can't credit this expression to Horace too. Indeed, far from having such impressive classical origins, as a stock phrase *carpe noctem* appears to have emerged as relatively recently as the nineteenth century, and as a snappy motto it has largely struggled to catch on and fails to make the pages of many dictionaries today. Those more exhaustive dictionaries that do list *carpe noctem* tend merely to interpret it as the literal companion to its more familiar cousin. While *carpe diem* advises us to make the most of the day ahead, *carpe noctem* is simply a motivator to work ceaselessly through the night.

But there is more to be gleaned here than simply an advertisement for candlelit study: by advocating working or acting while others are asleep, *carpe noctem* is a reminder not only to 'seize the night', but to seize *all* the time we have available to us – including that which we might usually be more inclined to ignore or to leave to tick by.

See also: eucatastrophe, opsimathy

CATACOSMESIS

≈

*for when you're feeling disorganised
or muddled*

If you're a muddle-headed, butterfly-minded, easily confused or disorganised person, then take heart – the dictionary proves you are by no means alone. In fact, it is so well furnished with words for bewildered thinkers and messy workers that the relatively few words it has for the opposite – the flawlessly clear-headed and effortlessly well organised – appear all the more conspicuous by their scarcity.

Originally a word for a butcher's assistant, a *dirty-gully*, for instance, is a messy, disorganised worker. An *ackermatut* (originally a Yorkshire regionalism for farm-yard manure) is a messy, disorganised room. A *cataclue* is 'a number of persons running in disorder and impeding each other', according to the *English Dialect Dictionary*.

A *huckmuck* is a jumbled mess, in which it is impossible to find anything you're looking for. To *maffle*, *hasther* or *scuddle* is to work in a messy, slapdash way. And *adhocracy* – a word perhaps more useful today than ever before – is a jocular 1960s invention for an informal management style that, in an attempt to reduce the need for bureaucracy, instead ends up acting erratically, inconsistently and hopelessly ineffectually.

We might not be alone in being disorganised, but that's not to say that we're happy to live up to our messy reputation. We could all do with being a little more focused and prepared every now and then, especially when we have a great deal of work thrown at us, or a vast number of tasks and chores to keep us busy. What we need, in fact, is *catacosmesis*.

Catacosmesis – literally 'arrangement' in Greek – is a term from rhetoric, used to refer to a memorable and highly effective trope in which a series of facts, points, dates, names, or any other similar data or statistics are intentionally ranked or organised by a speaker and presented to the audience in a specific order – alphabetical, chronological, numerical and so on, depending on the data involved. The implication in *catacosmesis* is that the data is reordered into the most effective and memorable way possible, transforming what might otherwise be a random list of dreary or easily confused facts and figures into a punchier, more attention-grabbing sequence.

Take *catacosmesis* out of its rhetorical context, and what we have is a word concerned purely with effective organisation. And if you're a natural *haffler* or *scuddler*, who is looking to tackle the *huckmuck* in your *ackermatut*, then this is precisely what you need.

Catacosmesis notably involves stacking the tasks at hand in whatever order best suits us. So let's not just dive straight into whatever task is most appealing, shelving the tougher or less pleasant jobs for later. And, certainly, let's not try tackling four or five jobs at once, and end up doing none of them particularly well. *Catacosmesis* tells us to take a moment to organise our minds. It tells us to figure out precisely what tasks and jobs we have to do, gauge what order it might be best to do them in and then check them off, simply and productively, one at a time. Less *cataclue* – more *catacosmesis*.

See also: cultellation, stravaig

CHALCENTROUS

≈

for when you're facing a challenge

Each of the words and chapters in this book are intended to address one of life's challenges, from grief and heartache, to stress, boredom, work troubles and homesickness. But what word can we turn to when we come across *any* challenge in our life, regardless of what has caused it?

One option is the wonderful word *philobat* – a relatively recent, mid-twentieth-century addition to our language, coined by the Hungarian psychologist Michael Balint. Today, Balint is best remembered as one of the co-founders of the Balint Society, an international organisation aimed at schooling and advancing the patient–doctor relationship. But, in 1955, he published a landmark paper in the field of psychoanalysis entitled *Friendly Expanses; Horrid Empty Spaces*, in which he introduced two newly defined character traits or personality types, differentiated by their relationships to the people and objects in their lives, and how they react to situations in which these familiar objects are not around.

On the one hand, Balint theorised, is the kind of person who tends as a rule to avoid difficult or unfamiliar situations, clinging to and heavily relying on familiar people, places and objects when these difficult times arise. The problem this type of character has, however, is that all of these familiar home comforts are isolated in a sea of 'horrid empty spaces', representative of all those situations and instances in which we are forced to act alone, without help or instruction from anyone else. This character – which Balint called the *ocnophil* ('hesitation lover' in Greek) – ultimately tries to spend as little time as possible in this empty space, preferring instead to rely on and be surrounded by comforting, familiar, unchallenging things.

Directly opposed to the *ocnophil* is the *philobat*. To the *philobat*, these 'horrid empty spaces' are actually 'friendly expanses' – a world filled with unfamiliar territory and awash with new possibilities and opportunities, simply waiting to be discovered and experienced. Just as was the case for the *ocnophil*, this expanse is peppered with familiar places, faces and things, but the *philobat* typically prefers to shun these comforts and instead relishes the prospect of facing the challenges of the wide-open space on their own. Indeed, in accounting for how he coined such an unusual word, Balint explained that just as '*acrobat* means literally "one who walks on his toes", i.e. away from the safe earth . . . I shall use "philobat" to describe one who enjoys such thrills'.

When facing the unexpected we must channel our inner *philobat*. If we're lucky, like the *ocnophil* we too shall have a world of familiar, helpful and comforting people and things around us on which to rely when times are hard. But at the same time, if life throws a challenge at us, then it is we who must find the strength to overcome it. And, once it is over and done with, hopefully there will still be a world of familiar and welcoming faces on the other side of it.

Saying that we need to channel our inner *philobat* is all well and good, of course, but that raises the question of *how* we are meant to find that inner strength. Perhaps we also need a word here for inner resilience, strength and power. Happily, the dictionary is once again on hand to help us out with more than a few inspirational words.

A *netherstone*, for instance, is a tough, resilient inner core – or, figuratively, the very basis of a person's strength or resilience. Dating from the 1500s, it describes the lower or 'nether' of a pair of millstones, against which the smaller, lighter, upper stone moves to mill the grain. The word *robust* literally means 'strong' and 'hardy' but its etymological root is more evocative: *robust* comes from *robus*, the Latin word for oak timber, and so to be *robust* is literally to be as irrepressibly tough and resilient as solid oak. The words *roborean* and *roboreous* – 'made of oak' – can likewise be taken to mean 'sturdy' or 'inflexible', while a *roborant* is a strengthening, restorative food or medicine.

As images for inner strength and resilience go, perhaps best of all is *chalcentrous*. Originally a nickname of the Ancient Greek scholar Didymus (who is said to have written so prolifically and indefatigably that he often forgot points he had made in earlier books and so contradicted himself in later ones), *chalcentrous* literally means 'having intestines made of bronze'. With inner strength like that, what can stop you?

See also: eustress, extravagate, high-mettle

CULTELLATION

≈

for when you're feeling overwhelmed

We all go through periods when it can feel as if we have too much on our plates. Work stresses, family worries, health concerns, financial woes – problems like these can all conspire to overwhelm and exhaust us, leaving us bewildered, run down and often at a loss how best to deal with them. It is for good reason then that the word *overwhelmed* literally means 'turned upside down': a perfect storm of troubles can indeed feel as though it has turned an ordinary day entirely on its head.

So what word can we rely on for times when our greatest burden is that we are simply overburdened? It may not seem the most likely candidate, but perhaps a long-forgotten, long-unused term from the world of geographical surveying is the one we need.

Cultellation was originally the name of a process whereby a height or distance — often over difficult terrain, such as the distance from the base to the peak of a mountain — could be measured not in one single stroke, but in a series of smaller, more manageable sections. A length of marked tape or chain would be held out horizontally, with a weighted blade or point hanging perpendicularly on a second chain beneath it, striking a point on the ground below. These two measurements — the horizontal and the vertical — would then be recorded, and the process repeated once more from the point on the earth struck by the dangling blade. A second set of measurements would then be taken, then a third and fourth, and so on, until the entire distance had been covered in these incremental steps.

Adding together all the individual horizontal measurements would give the total distance, and adding together all the perpendicular lengths measured by the blade would give the total height. In fact, it is this dangling blade (as well as perhaps the notion of 'slicing' the longer distance into smaller pieces) that hints at the word's origins in *cultellus*, a Latin word for a small knife.

The kinds of problems we have on our proverbial plates today, admittedly, aren't likely to be the same as those faced by seventeenth-century surveyors, but there is more to this word than meets the eye.

Borrowed into English from French, the word *cultellation* first appeared in the language in this original, strictly practical sense in the mid sixteenth century. Over time, however, it began to be used more loosely, so that by the mid 1700s it had come to refer more generally to the piecemeal solving of any intricate or difficult problem, by breaking it down into smaller, more manageable and more readily resolvable constituent parts. From those fairly dreary beginnings, ultimately, *cultellation* has become a word to remind us that when we are overwhelmed with worries or chores – or, indeed, one single seemingly impenetrable task – breaking down our problems into smaller sections can make them more tractable, less daunting and more manageable.

See also: catacosmesis, gadwaddick, stravaig, violon d'ingres

DOLORIFUGE

≈

for when you're overcome with sadness

For such a simple and seemingly unassuming word, *sad* packs quite a punch. Its brevity and simplicity belies the fact that sadness itself can be exhausting and incapacitating, and is often potent enough to change your entire outlook on life, muddle your thought processes and hold you back from being yourself.

Even in terms of its etymology, *sad* still rather punches above its weight, as hidden behind it is quite a complex and lengthy linguistic history. Its roots lie in its Old English equivalent *sæd*, but unlike its modern descendant, *sæd* was a somewhat positive word, used to mean 'satisfied', 'well-sated' or, by extension, 'solid', 'heavy' or 'steadfast'. Over time those original meanings shifted into ever more negative territory: 'well-sated' came to mean 'having overindulged', or 'having become

weary of something', while as another word for stead-
fastness or solidity, *sad* began to develop connotations of
seriousness, gravity and heavy-heartedness. By the 1400s
these more negative senses had begun to dominate, and
as the earlier, more positive meanings of *sad* began to
die away, the word finally began to resemble the *sadness*
we have in our language today. *Sad* has ultimately been
used to mean 'sorrowful' or 'miserable' since the early
sixteenth century.

That lengthy history proves that *sadness* is neither
nothing new, nor anything uncommon. We all feel
sad from time to time and the melancholic feelings of
dejectedness and dispiritedness that sadness brings with
it are universal. Proof, if it were ever needed, that we are
never alone in our saddest moments lies in the fact that
the dictionary even provides us with a word – *collugency*
– for mutual sadness, or the act of mourning together.

But while sadness itself might be familiar to us all,
the causes (and therefore the cures) of all of our individual sadnesses differ from person to person, and are
as varied as the words our language has developed to
describe them. *Lonesome-fret*, for instance, is sadness
sparked by loneliness or solitude. *Merry-go-sorry* is a long-
forgotten word for a melancholic mixture of happiness
and sadness; its French equivalent *chantepleure* (adopted

into English as far back as the 1400s) literally means 'singing and crying'.

To feel *dowffy* is to feel lethargic with downheart-edness. To be *sullen-sick* is to make yourself physically unwell with some inner emotional turmoil. And, back in the sixteenth century, saying that you were in your *mubble-fubbles* meant that you were just generally feel-ing down, or out of sorts – or, as an 1846 *Dictionary of Archaic and Provincial Words* astutely defined it, 'depressed in spirits, without any serious cause'.

Alas, there is no silver bullet that can magically cure all these different forms of sadness. Resolving our despondency instead relies on isolating whatever it was that sparked it in the first place and fixing whatever the problem may have been. The closest we have to a lin-guistic cure-all is a *dolorifuge*.

Dolor was a Latin word for pain or grief, and ety-mologically it lies at the root of a number of words in the dictionary relating to sadness or mental anguish. Most familiar of these is likely *dolorous* and *dolorousness*, which emerged in English in the fifteenth and sixteenth centuries respectively. Their root form, *dolour*, a word meaning 'sorrow' or 'suffering', is nowadays relatively rare, as are a number of other less familiar words in this downhearted group, including *dolorimeter* (a device for measuring a person's sensitivity to pain), *doloroso* (a musical term directing a performer to play in a plaintive, mournful fashion) and *dolorifuge*, which combines that same Latin root, *dolor*, with the verb *fugere*, meaning 'to flee' (the same root as *fugitive*, and *refuge*).

A *dolorifuge* is anything that works to expel or rid you of sadness, anguish or pain. Quite what form that takes depends on you and the particular upsetting circumstances in which you find yourself. Sadness triggered by missing home and familiar faces, for instance, might be mended by little more than a reassuring phone call, or a glance at a much loved photograph. Sadness caused by grief, or heartache, might need a more robust approach, and the support of a circle of friends and family. Even in the most desperate of circumstances it might just be possible to imagine an appropriate and curative *dolorifuge*.

See also: growlery, respair

DRUERY

≋

for when a relationship is ending

The chances are that anyone who has been in a romantic relationship is likely to have endured the end of a romantic relationship. Whether the parting is mutual and clean or tearful and messy, such times are always difficult, not least because of the mixture of feelings and emotions. Sadness that your time together is over mingles uneasily with memories of happiness and gratitude for shared good times. Similarly, regret for past mistakes or time ill spent shades into nervous excitement, eagerness for a fresh start and some much-needed headspace. Our everyday lives often change after a break-up too. We're forced to make new connections and explore uncharted territory – all without someone we once cared deeply for at our side.

Relationships can be brief or longer-lasting, can dwindle to a natural conclusion or be wrenched painfully apart. But however they play out, navigating our way out of them is one of life's many challenges. The old adage that time heals is usually appropriate here: the initial shock or hurt of a break-up eventually diminishes as we begin to build, and then become better accustomed to, whatever the next chapter in our life will be. But the relationship now behind us doesn't just simply disappear. As with all life experiences, we learn and grow from it – and in doing so, take a little bit of every past relationship, every break-up and every partner with us through our lives. There's a beautiful word for precisely that.

A *druery* is a love token, or a treasured memento. Derived from *drut*, an Old French word for a lover or a much loved companion, *druery* was originally used in much the same way as that in English, when it first appeared in the language back in the thirteenth century. Over time, however, that meaning expanded onto more material things, and *druery* eventually transformed into a word for a gift or keepsake from a lover, or anything held precious or much prized.

In some dialects, that development continued unchecked; in Scots, for instance, *druery* came to be confused with *dowry*, and from there was mistakenly used to refer to all those material things that pass from one spouse to another on marriage. But it is the word's earlier and considerably more romantic meaning that concerns us here.

As a word for a keepsake from a lover, *druery* can of course still be interpreted solely in material terms. When a relationship ends, we might still have photographs, keepsakes, letters and messages to hold dear and look back on. More figuratively, *druery* can also be interpreted as a handy word for all those memories and lessons we take from our previous relationships and carry with us throughout the rest of our lives. If a relationship ends on good terms, we can take heart from it, and recall its past memories and *drueries* fondly. Even if a relationship ends badly, we can still use it and its *drueries* positively, to build strength and resilience, to help gather our thoughts and learn from our past experiences, and ultimately build better and richer connections in the future. Whether born out of good or bad experiences, these *drueries* nevertheless make us who we are, and are carried with us for the rest of our lives.

See also: anacampserote, redamancy

EUCATASTROPHE

≈

for when you're feeling pessimistic

While the optimist likes to look positively to the future, the pessimist worries about the unknown, and fears the constant potential for calamity or tragedy. If you're naturally something of a pessimist, then snapping out of that way of thinking can be more easily said than done. The more hopeful you are, the pessimist thinks, the worse it will feel when those hopes are inevitably dashed – because after all, disaster and failure are surely lurking around every corner.

It is true that we can never know what the future has in store for us. But what the pessimist forgets by embracing the constant threat of catastrophe, is that there is always the equally constant potential for a *eucatastrophe*.

Derived from a Greek word for 'good', that initial *eu–* in *eucatastrophe* is a familiar prefix in English, used

to form words bearing some sense of positivity, favour-
ability or worthiness. So *euphony* is pleasant sound. A
euphemism is a more acceptable phrasing of a questionable concept. A *eucalyptus* tree is literally 'well-covered'
in leaves. And that initial *eu-* is often employed to create
words acting as opposites or counterparts for other more
negative equivalents. The opposite of 'dysfunction' is
eufunction. The opposite of 'dyspepsia' is *eupepsia*. The
opposite of 'stress' is EUSTRESS. And the opposite of a
'catastrophe', quite simply, is a *eucatastrophe*.

The word *catastrophe* itself comes from a Greek word
meaning 'to overturn'. Originally it was a literary or
theatrical term used to refer a dramatic upheaval in a
plotline that brings about or hastens the conclusion of a
story, and it was from this early notion of a tumultuous
and often unexpected event that the word eventually
came to be used in the early eighteenth century of any
sudden, unforeseen or extensive disaster. Based on this
notion of an entirely unforeseen disaster, *Lord of the Rings*
author J. R. R. Tolkien invented the word *eucatastrophe*
to act as its wholly positive counterpart.

In 1939, Tolkien was invited to give a lecture on the
history of fairy-tales at the University of St Andrews in
Scotland. Although the text of Tolkien's original lecture is lost, two years later he returned to the subject

by chance in a letter to his then twenty-year-old son Christopher. Writing that he had recently heard a sermon in church about a child who had been miraculously cured of tuberculosis at a healing spa in France, Tolkien explained that he had been 'deeply moved' by the story, and had felt a 'peculiar emotion . . . quite unlike any other sensation' he had experienced before. 'All of a sudden,' he continued, 'I realised what it was: the very thing that I have been trying to write about, and explain in that fairy-story essay . . . For it, I coined the word "eucatastrophe": the sudden happy turn in a story, which pierces you with a joy that brings tears.'

In 1947, Tolkien finally adapted his St Andrews lecture into an article entitled 'On Fairy Stories', in which he expanded on this idea of a wholly positive and fortuitous 'turn' of events. Moments like these, he wrote, offer 'a piercing glimpse of joy and heart's desire', and when one turns up in the plot of a book or film, it 'for a moment passes outside the frame, rends indeed the very web of story, and lets a gleam come through'.

So, while a *catastrophe* is a grand, unexpected disaster, a *eucatastrophe* is an equally unexpected but entirely wonderful change of circumstances. It reminds us not merely to focus on the chance of some future disaster, but on the opportunities presented by a sudden and entirely positive shift or event. There need not be a catastrophe lurking around the corner, then, but a *eucatastrophe*.

See also: agathism, carpe noctem, eustress, interfulgent, meliorism, the worse the passage, the more welcome the port

EUSTRESS

≋

for when you're feeling stressed

The etymological story behind the word *stress* is a particularly telling one. *Stress* is a clipped form of *distress*, a slightly older word that dates back to the 1200s. It in turn was adopted into English from French, but its roots lie in an ancient Latin verb, *stringere*, that was variously used to mean 'to push', 'to tighten' or 'to compress'. That makes *stress* a distant cousin of words such as *restrict*, *constrict*, *astringent* and *constraint*. All those related words seem particularly apt in talking about stress. Stress can constrain our lives, making us feel trapped and compressed, and the panic and anxiety that so often accompanies it can restrict our lives even more.

The occasional stressful situation is tolerable and can in fact prove motivating and energising. But living through day after day of stress is more dangerous, and is good for neither our mental nor our physical health. Tackling whatever problem is causing the stress is important; finding the right help and advice when we need it can stave off the very worst that a stressful life can throw at us.

If all we need is a helping hand through the occasional stressful period, however, there is a word we can turn to for a little guidance and reassurance. Just as a EUCATASTROPHE is the positive counterpart to a disastrous *catastrophe*, *eustress* is the positive counterpart to *stress*, or *distress*.

Unlike the word *stress* (the origins of which lie way back in the Middle English period), *eustress* is a twentieth-century invention, coined by a Hungarian physician named Hans Selye as recently as 1964. Although we think of stress as a psychological concept, Selye was primarily an endocrinologist and his concept of *eustress* developed from his work studying the body's chemical and biological responses to stressful situations. Stress, he theorised, could be divided into one of two distinct forms, depending on how the body responded to it, and whether or not the body returned to its normal unstressed state once the stressful situation had passed.

Longer-term, largely negative, stress – which cannot readily be coped with or adapted to – he termed *distress*, and it is this form of stress that can cause anxiety and mental anguish, and have grossly detrimental effects on our overall well-being. On the other hand, however, there is positive and motivating stress, which Selye termed *eustress*. This stress compels us to perform better or faster, he suggested, or to operate at a higher level than we might otherwise manage to do in an unstressed state.

Some situations can muddy this distinction. *Distress* can come hand in hand with *eustress* if its effect is to lead us to create our own positive outcomes, such as becoming more resilient or devising coping mechanisms. Moreover, Selye's two categories are by no means universal: a situation that might spark *eustress* in one person might send another into a dangerous spiral of *distress*. But when we face a stressful situation or period in our lives, merely knowing that this distinction even exists – and, for that matter, that the word *eustress* itself is there in our language – can be something of a reassurance.

What the word *eustress* tells us is that stress need not always be debilitating and disastrous. *Eustress* can inspire us to embrace an occasional jolt outside our comfort zone – albeit alongside all the nervousness and apprehension that comes with it.

See also: chalcentrous, eucatastrophe

EXTRAVAGATE

≈

*for when you're feeling bored
or lacking a challenge*

A few pages back, under AUTOSCHEDIASM, we found out how the oddly macabre breeding behaviour of a wasp had improbably given us a word for a feeling of being stuck in a robotic rut. But in some instances it's not our routine that makes our life boring, and nor is it a sudden jolt of spontaneity that we really need. Sometimes, what we need is a fresh challenge, something different: a new skill to acquire or a new focus for our ambitions. Sometimes what is keeping us bored is simply that we have allowed ourselves to become boring. And if that's the case, then perhaps the time has come to *extravagate*.

No doubt that word looks somewhat familiar thanks to its older and better-known etymological cousin *extravagant*, which has been with us in the language since Middle English times. Back then, *extravagant* was a somewhat more weighty word than it is today, specifically applied to papal decrees and constitutions that had not been fully codified, and so existed outside religious law; the word *extravagant* itself literally means a 'wandering outside'. Via the Latin verb *vagare*, 'to roam', it is a none-too distant relative of words such as *vagrancy* and *vagabond*. By the fifteenth century that meaning had begun to broaden, and the adjective *extravagant* had come to be applied to anything at all that simply 'strays' or 'wanders' outside of the ordinary. That paved the way for the meaning we have today, and, in the early seventeenth century, also inspired the related verb *extravagate*.

Originally, *extravagate* was also used fairly specifically, to refer to the act of wandering from a text or stock set of rules, or digressing from the point of a conversation. Over time, it too came to be used more broadly, and by the mid 1700s had come to be used to mean 'to wander or roam at will', or beyond the normal limits or boundaries. *Extravagate* is ultimately a word for pushing beyond that which is ordinary or expected, and out into uncharted, unpredictable territory. If we're lacking a challenge or feeling bored by what we have around us every day, then *extravagating* can provide the impetus we need to find something different to break out of our routine, and set our sights on some new and more exciting goal.

See also: chalcentrous

FROWST

≈

for when you're feeling exhausted

When you have tired yourself out with sport or exercise, feeling exhausted can be strangely invigorating. When you're worn out from a long slog at work, or a race to study for an exam or hit a deadline, exhaustion is less energising, but the rest that it demands will at least feel well earned. But when you're exhausted simply from being worn down or overwhelmed by troubles and stresses, that is something quite different.

No matter *why* you're feeling run down, the solution is often the same: we need to take the time to be kind to ourselves, reward our efforts with some much needed self-indulgence, and find the time to rest and recharge our batteries. And the dictionary gives us plenty of linguistic ammunition to do just that.

When it comes to indulging yourself, a word well

worth living by is *abligurition*, an eighteenth-century term for excessive spending on food and drink (or, as the 1724 dictionary that first defined it put it, 'a prodigal spending in belly-cheer'). A *roborant*, likewise, is a hearty, restorative food or meal, while to *swage* is to lounge around and relax after you have eaten your fill. A *supernaculum* is a drink so delicious that you savour it to its very last drop – but if you don't quite have the time for that, then you've surely got time for a *whiss*, a tiny invigorating sip of warming liquor.

If you have earned a reward, then you can indulge your *sybaritic* side too. Sybaris was the name of an Ancient Greek city in the south of modern-day Italy, whose inhabitants had a reputation among the other Greek peoples for their love of luxury and extravagance. A *sybarite*, ultimately, is someone who follows the same lifestyle – as, for that matter, is an *akolast*. Derived from a Greek word meaning 'unruly' or 'dissolute', *akolast* – meaning 'pleasure-seeker' or 'hedonist' – was adopted into English in the sixteenth century thanks to *Akolastus*, the title of a popular play of the time retelling the biblical story of the Prodigal Son.

You can indulge yourself in more than food and drink, of course, and so while you're making the most of your leisure time, you might wish to *popjoy* – a nineteenth-century word for entertaining yourself with some frivolous pastime or hobby. The word *hobby-horse* itself can also be used as a verb, meaning simply 'to entertain yourself with something you enjoy', while the happiness you experience from doing it is known as *joyance*. If you're a reader, *to meditate the Muse* is a seventeenth-century phrase meaning 'to lose oneself in reading or poetry'. And if you're more of a music-lover, to *glad-warble* is to sing purely for pleasure, while the joy that comes from listening to music was charmingly known as *glee-dream* in Old English. If you're looking to wind down at the end of a tough day, then music that is *hesychastic* is probably more what you're looking for: derived from a Greek word meaning 'to be still' or 'to keep quiet', *hesychastic* music calms the spirit and soothes the mind.

Then again, perhaps all you need to recharge your batteries is a good night's sleep. To *snoozle* is to lie snugly in a comfortable place. To *lurdge* is to indulge in laziness. A *sloum* is a brief nap. And the lovely word *snerdle*, according to the *English Dialect Dictionary*, can be used to mean 'to nestle closely', 'to wrap up comfortably in bed' or 'to go comfortably off to sleep'.

If, even after a good night's sleep, you're still not feeling sufficiently recovered, there's *frowst* – a superbly useful word from nineteenth-century slang for a lie-in on Sunday mornings.

According to the *Oxford English Dictionary*, *frowst* or *froust* first emerged in the colloquial jargon of students at Harrow School in north-west London, one of the oldest and most prestigious independent schools in England. In fact, the word's earliest known record comes from a biographical account written by one of the school's former pupils, *Hugh Russell at Harrow: A Sketch of School Life*, published in 1880. In 'a glossary of some of the words and uses of words peculiar to Harrow' included as an appendix to Russell's *Sketch*, the word *frowst* was defined as 'extra time in bed on Sundays, saints' days, and whole holidays'. (The same glossary also helpfully recorded that a comfortable armchair was known as a *frouster*.)

As for precisely where the word *frowst* itself comes from, we can presume that it's simply a development of the earlier adjective *frowsty*, which has been used to mean 'fusty', 'stale' or 'musty' since the early nineteenth century. *Frowsty* in turn is probably related to a host of earlier and similar words including *frowish*, which has been in use since the seventeenth century, and *frowzy* (meaning 'ill-ventilated') and *froughty* (meaning 'stale' or 'spoiled'), both of which date back as far as the

mid 1500s. When you are in dire need of some extra
rest, perhaps *frowst* is exactly the word you are looking for.

See also: hurkle-durkle, self-soothe

GADWADDICK

≋

for when you're feeling work-weary

For as long as people have worked, people have worked too hard. And as if we ever needed proof of that, all we'd need to do would be to look in the dictionary.

There's a whole family of words that first started to emerge in the language more than a thousand years ago. Back then, English began to develop a prefix, *for-*, that was used to build words bearing some sense of doing something so utterly, so extremely or so thoroughly that the current state of affairs is entirely altered. A handful of these words still exists today (*forgive*, *forbid* and *forsake* among them), but the vast majority have long since fallen by the linguistic wayside. Regrettably, that means that we now have to make do without such exquisitely useful terms as *forslug* ('to neglect something through laziness'), *forgab* ('to circulate defamations about someone') and *forglut* ('to devour completely').

As time went by *for-* began to be used in ever more figurative and inventive ways – including building words implying some sense of doing or experiencing something to such an unwelcome degree that you are left utterly exhausted or overwhelmed by it. To be *forwallowed*, for instance, is to be worn out from a restless night's sleep. To be *forfasted* is to be exhausted by dieting. Someone who is *forfoughten* is fatigued from fighting or arguing. And, if you are left utterly exhausted by your work, you can be *fortoiled*, *fortravailed*, *forlaboured* and *forswunk*. The earliest of all these, *forswunk* (derived from an Old English word, *swink*, for laborious or difficult work), was first recorded in a collection of proverbs compiled sometime in the late twelfth century. Being worn out by the tasks you have at hand is not only a contemporary problem.

Not that exhaustion is the only work-related problem the dictionary can help us name. As well as being *forlaboured* and *forswunk*, to be *dwanged* is to be oppressed with too much work. As we have already found out (under ALLABORATE), to *wurdle* is to work hard on something, despite knowing that it has little chance of success. To *shaffle* is to work in a disorganised or half-hearted way and a *duntabout*, inspired by an old word for a wooden staff or 'dunt' used as a makeshift target, is an over-worked employee.

To get into Friday-street is to fall behind on your work or to leave everything until the last moment. As the final day of the working week, Friday has long been used in the names of places to imply some sense of an ending or boundary, and hence *Friday-street* is an age-old nickname for either the outermost limit of an area of woodland, or else an isolated row of houses on the furthest outskirts of a village. Any such street would typically represent a traveller's last opportunity to purchase supplies or ask for directions before heading out onto the open road, and so *coming into Friday-street* came to imply leaving much of your work to be completed at the latest possible time.

The ancient proverb *a bow, long bent, grows weak* advises that workers who are stressed or overburdened cannot be expected to work to their full potential, and will over time lose their keenness and consistency. A reference to the gradual weakening of archers' bows, this saying was first recorded in English in the mid sixteenth century – but the sentiment behind can be traced back more than two and a half thousand years. 'They . . . who have a bow bend it only at the time they want it,' advised the Ancient Greek historian Herodotus. 'It is precisely the same with a man – if, without some intervals of amusement, he applied himself constantly to serious pursuits, he would imperceptibly lose his vigour both of mind and body.'

If you have ever worked for someone who sees no issue in dropping vast to-do lists onto their staff at the last moment – or anywhere where piles of unwanted work are passed from person to person (before typically landing on the desk of whoever is least equipped to deal with them) – then *to finish Aladdin's window* is another expression of work-weariness well worth remembering. It derives from a curious episode in an eighteenth-century retelling of Aladdin's story, in which Aladdin has his genie construct an enormous palace – gaudier and even more impressive than the sultan's – in order to prove both his wealth and his suitability to marry the princess. Set into the walls of the palace are two dozen ornate window niches, all but one of which are decorated with innumerable emeralds, diamonds, sapphires, rubies and countless other precious stones. When the sultan is invited to visit Aladdin's palace, he spots this curiously unfinished corner and, as a means of proving his own affluence and benevolence to his daughter's suitor, offers to have his staff complete Aladdin's work for him.

Despite calling on his best jewellers and goldsmiths to carry out the work, however, the sultan and his team simply cannot match the splendour of the other window niches, and with his treasury emptied of its finest treasures, the sultan is forced to abandon the job halfway. Aladdin ultimately has the sultan's attempt dismantled, returns his jewels to him and calls on his genie to use his magic to complete the niche instead. When the sultan returns and sees the finished product, he is astonished, and enthusiastically grants his blessing to the marriage of his daughter and Aladdin.

It is the sultan's inability to complete what Aladdin had started – despite his very best efforts, and all his resources – that lies at the root of this expression. *To finish Aladdin's window* is to be tasked with completing something left unfinished by a superior, which in practice proves far beyond your capabilities.

It's unlikely your work these days will involve completing jewel-encrusted window niches, of course, but that's not to say that work is now any less taxing or challenging. Unfortunately, it's equally unlikely that any of us have a magical genie to complete our work for us. As it is, we can all feel a little stressed and wearied with work – or a little *forswunk* – and in need of some help and encouragement to get through it.

If you're feeling a little wearied by your work or your workload, perhaps the best remedy is just a break from it all. Some much needed rest, relaxation and reinvigoration. Perhaps all you need is to *gadwaddick*.

According to the *English Dialect Dictionary*, to *gadwaddick* is 'to jaunt' or 'to go on a pleasure trip'. Quite where a word as unusual as *gadwaddick* comes from is anyone's guess; neither the *English Dialect Dictionary* nor any of the other dictionaries that list it appear to offer any clues, and the most likely explanation is that it is somehow distantly derived from the same root (or else is some local corruption of) the more familiar word *gallivant*. The origins of *gadwaddicking*, however, aren't quite so important to us here as what it represents: simply taking a break away from it all.

It's all too easy to allow our professional lives to overshadow everything else and, as Herodotus pointed out, no one can be expected to work to their full potential if their work is wearing them down. Every so often, we all need to switch off, recuperate and return to work refreshed and re-energised.

Not all of us have the luxury of time off. For a great many of us these days, our workloads and schedules make the idea of downing tools and getting away from it all, even for just a short time, next to impossible.

We might not have time to fit a *gadwaddick* into our schedule, but how about *sproguing* – a Scots and North Country word for a leisurely head-clearing walk in the countryside? Another Scots word is at the root of the equally pertinent expression *to make causey-webs*: a *causey* is a street or road, and this delightful nineteenth-century invention means 'to neglect your work and idle in the streets'. You can also turn to STRAVAIGING or a recuperative VILLEGGIATURA for the city-weary.

For anyone just looking for an easy end to a challenging day perhaps the best word for you is an obscure English dialect invention, *powl* – defined by an 1850 guide to the *Dialect of South Lancashire* as 'to leave off work, and go to the alehouse'.

See also: cultellation, violon d'ingres

GROWLERY

≈

for when you're in a bad mood

Even the most even-tempered of people can find themselves in a bad mood every so often. Luckily, there's a rich vocabulary of words to describe precisely that.

If you're *zowerzopped*, for instance, then you're crabbily ill-natured or in a bad mood – at least according to an 1837 guide to the *Devonshire Dialect*, which also helpfully points out this peculiar-looking word literally means 'sour-sapped'. To *sumph* is to sulk or grumble tetchily, as is to *glunch* and to *mulp*, while to *drunt* is to take a huff. As well as being a dialect word for a disdainful shrug of the shoulders, a *himps* is also a bad mood, as is both a *struckle* and, according to the *Scottish National Dictionary*, a *bocksturrocks* (precisely where that brilliant word comes from is a complete mystery).

Bad moods are even found hidden inside the histories of some of the words in our language. The word *boudoir* derives from the French verb *bouder*, meaning 'to pout' or 'sulk' – which makes this classiest of words for a private chamber 'a room for sulking'. And although it'll be much more familiar to English speakers as an adjective, as a noun a *sulky* is a type of horse-drawn carriage dating from the eighteenth century. As this particular style of carriage accommodated only a single solitary passenger, it was the perfect mode of transport for someone who petulantly and sulkily wanted to be left alone. It was also known by a French name, *desobligeant*, literally meaning 'disobliging', or 'standoffish'.

Bad moods pass eventually, but in the meantime we might feel as though we need a little time to ourselves – though the chances of us having a horse-drawn carriage to retire to are probably fairly slim. Instead, what we need is a *growlery*.

Like so many of the English language's best and most inventive words, *growlery* is a word we owe to one of our best and most inventive writers. In 1853, Charles Dickens used the word *growlery* in his novel *Bleak House*. As the kindly benefactor Mr Jarndyce welcomes one of the novel's key narrators, Esther Summerson, to his eponymous home, he shows her into 'a small room next his bed-chamber', containing 'a little library of books and papers, and in part quite a little museum of his boots and shoes and hat-boxes'.

> 'Sit down, my dear,' said Mr Jarndyce. 'This, you must know, is the growlery. When I am out of humour, I come and growl here.'
>
> 'You must be here very seldom, sir,' said I.
>
> 'Oh, you don't know me!' he returned. 'When I am deceived or disappointed . . . I take refuge here. The growlery is the best-used room in the house.'

Although the word *growlery* itself had first appeared in the language somewhat earlier (as a term for the sound of grumbling or complaining) Mr Jarndyce's *growlery* is essentially the Dickensian equivalent of what we in our less poetic, twenty-first-century language might call a 'safe space'. It is a calming, comfortable, solitary room, filled with familiar and enlightening things, in which a bad mood can be privately vented, mused on and assuaged.

We might not all have the luxury of a bespoke room in a rambling country retreat in which to give vent to our problems, but there's no reason why our own particular *growleries* have to match Mr Jarndyce's. Perhaps your favourite place to be when you're *zowerzopped* or feeling in a *bocksturrocks* is on a lonely walk in the fresh air. Perhaps it's a hot bath, or sitting with a good book in a cosy chair. Or perhaps your favoured way of righting your mood is to set the world to rights over a drink or two in the local pub. Wherever – or, for that matter, whatever – your particular *growlery* is, it's undoubtedly a word and a place well worth knowing whenever you need to lighten your spirits.

See also: dolorifuge

HEAFGANG

≋

for when you're feeling homesick

Although we use it to mean merely 'a sentimental longing', the word *nostalgia* was originally used of homesickness. At its root are two Greek words, *nostos*, meaning a homecoming or homeward-bound journey, and *algos*, a Greek word for pain.

Given that somewhat surprising etymology, it's perhaps understandable to find that *nostalgia* was also originally considered potent enough to be classified as a medical condition. 'The concourse of depressing symptoms which sometimes arise in persons who are absent from their native country,' as one Victorian medical dictionary described it, 'when they are seized with a longing desire of returning to their home and friends, and the scenes of their youth.' Everything from fever to insomnia to dysentery, skin lesions and even incontinence were listed among the symptoms of this medical *nostalgia*, which physicians of the day postulated might be caused by atmospheric differences, between the various locations in which we find ourselves, upsetting the body's delicate chemistry.

The English language – and, for that matter, our understanding of the role our psychology plays in our physical health – has changed a lot since the nineteenth century. As a consequence, use of the word *nostalgia* has long since weakened and this kind of intense, debilitating, medically significant homesickness is now properly known as *nostomania*. But while the language has moved on, the fact that homesickness is still one of the most intensely upsetting emotions – and arguably one of the most difficult to overcome – has not.

Experiencing homesickness can be a positive thing, as it shows just how much we care for the people we miss, and the strength of our connection to our home and our home life. Simply reconnecting to, or revisiting, our home and our friends and family there is as sure-fire a cure for homesickness as there could ever be. But part of what makes homesickness such a difficult emotion to overcome is that returning home is not always immediately possible, if indeed possible at all.

Sometimes we find ourselves stuck far away from

home, bound to a job or position we cannot abandon, or scuppered by a lack of transport, thereby making any journey home all but impracticable. Even worse, sometimes we can find ourselves missing, or longing for, somewhere or someone that is no longer there, in which case our homesickness might prove all but impossible to dispel.

Perhaps because this is such a potent mix of sadness, wistfulness, anguish and grief, words describing homesickness – and of feeling isolated in an unfamiliar place, overcome with unfamiliar surroundings, or missing the familiar, comforting sights and sounds of home – are surprisingly numerous in the language. In nineteenth-century English, it was known as *mother-sickness*, perhaps a reference to missing one's 'motherland', just as much as one's family. Before then, it was *country disease* or *country distemper* or, even more specifically, the *Swiss disease*, in reference to it supposedly being particularly prevalent among soldiers serving abroad with the Swiss army.

Somewhat ironically for a word concerned with being away from home, English has picked up a handful of words for a wistful longing for home from a number of other languages. The Irish *aduantas* describes the upset or unease of being somewhere unfamiliar, or surrounded by people you do not know. *Hiraeth* is a Welsh word essentially describing an intense longing to return to somewhere now gone, or that perhaps never was, or else a grief felt when someone is lost, changing familiar circumstances beyond repair. Often more poetically explained as 'a longing to return to where your spirit belongs', *hiraeth* is (for good reason) often found on lists of words that are supposedly impossible to translate precisely into English.

Dépaysé and *déraciné* are a pair of French loanwords adopted into English in the early 1900s. The former (derived from the French word for 'country', *pays*) literally describes the uneasy or unsettling feeling of being in a foreign and unfamiliar land, or more loosely, any feeling of upset caused by being in an unfamiliar place; the discomfort or homesickness that accompanies just such a situation is likewise known as *dépaysment*. *Déraciné*, meanwhile, is used to mean 'displaced' or 'exiled' – or, given that it derives from the French word for a plant's root, *racine*, the feeling of literally being 'uprooted'.

Homesickness is often sparked or worsened by the tantalising prospect of going home, or by at long last reaching the end of a tiresome homeward journey. The final, seemingly unending mile of just such a journey is known as a *wheady-mile*, according to the *English Dialect Dictionary*, which defines the adjective *wheady*, or *wady*, as meaning 'tedious', 'interminable' or (as is perhaps more the case here) 'containing more than was expected'. In nineteenth-century slang, just such a feeling was known as *channel fever* – although a quick glance through the dictionary shows that that name was not always so used.

Originally, *channel fever* was a naval nickname for an apparent malady supposedly suffered by workshy new recruits who, having been full of enthusiasm for the their new life at sea while still on dry land, would fall foul of a mysterious malaise – grave enough to see them excused from their maritime duties – as soon as they were aboard ship and had discovered just how arduous naval life actually was. The name itself began as a droll reference to the fact that these new recruits' zeal for a life on the ocean wave would typically disappear before they had even left the English Channel. But by the turn of the century, *channel fever* had come to be applied to a quite different feeling in British Navy slang.

After a long time away at sea or at war, wearied sailors and crew members would begin to feel a surge of homesickness as their vessel finally neared home waters. With their lives and loved ones now tantalisingly close, an aching combination of restless excitement and nervous melancholy would afflict even the oldest and saltiest of seadogs. As this phenomenon became more common and ever more noticeable, it soon required a name: the old term was simply recycled, and so it is this particular brand of homesickness – worsened by a long journey and sparked by its imminent end – that is now known as *channel fever.*

If we *are* able to go home, then our homesickness can easily be dispelled by doing so – or even by the promise of an eventual journey home. In other words, with a *heafgang.*

Heaf is a sixteenth-century word for an area of farmland pasture, and in particular the normal pasture to which an animal or herd of animals is familiar or well accustomed. In that sense, *heaf* is thought to be a local English corruption of another equally obscure word, *haft*, meaning 'to fix a living quarters' or 'to establish a home'. The derivative *heafgang* first appeared sometime around the early 1800s; if a *heaf* is an area to which one is well accustomed, then a *heafgang* – literally a 'heaf-going' – is the journey that leads us back there.

Like *heaf* itself, *heafgang* was originally used only in agricultural contexts to refer to the driving home of livestock (in particular, sheep in hill farms and crofts) back onto their usual grazing lands. From that initial meaning, it did not take long for *heafgang* to be applied more figuratively to people suffering homesickness – and ultimately a *heafgang* became a word for any journey that takes us, at long last, back to the comfortingly familiar people and places of home.

If we're trying to dispel homesickness, then a *heaf-gang* is almost certain to cure us. But if going home *isn't* possible, what then? What can we take from a word literally meaning 'to go home', if the one thing we cannot do – despite endlessly longing to do so – is to go home? For that, we need to return to the word *heaf* itself.

As well as meaning simply 'familiar pasture', *heaf* also established itself as a verb in nineteenth-century English, meaning 'to lodge', 'to remain in place' or, more importantly, 'to make oneself at home'. If our circumstances have changed and home is no longer where or what it used to be, *heaf* is a word to remind us that as new and unfamiliar as these emergent circumstances might feel at the moment, with time they too will begin to feel like home. And until that happens, we can warm ourselves with whatever thoughts and memories of home we need.

Perhaps in the harshest and most upsetting of homesicknesses, then, we don't need a *heafgang* or a restorative journey home. We just need to make ourselves feel at home wherever we now are.

See also: antipelargy, howffy, minding

HIGH-METTLE

≈

for when you're lacking courage

Long before people fully understood the internal workings of the human body, the liver – as the largest of the body's visceral organs – was considered the source of all our passionate and most spirited emotions. It was also wrongly presumed that the liver was responsible for producing and storing the body's blood supply, and so any disease or injury to the liver was believed to directly affect the blood, and ultimately change our moods and emotions. As a result, love, jealousy, anger, bitterness and courage were all variously held to be under the direct influence of the liver and its chemistry.

This erroneous belief is recorded in a number of age-old phrases and expressions, a handful of which survive today. *To hang your liver on something*, for instance, was to desire it very earnestly. *To steal the liver from someone's belly* was to take their heart or make them fall madly in love with you. To be *hot-livered* in sixteenth-century English was to be excitable or quick-tempered, while to be *cold-livered* was to be passionless. Likewise, to be *white-livered* was to be utterly lacking courage – as the blood could appear to drain from the liver, leaving its owner insipidly weak and cowardly. *Lily-livered*, a reference to the flower's fiercely white petals, is the more usual term for cowardice today.

We have an imaginative term for a lack of courage, then, but what about its opposite? What word can we turn to for inspiration when we need to summon up all our courage, and act as bravely or audaciously as we can?

In seventeenth-century English, to *commasculate* was to act courageously, or to instil bravery. Unsurprisingly, it derives from the same root as the word *masculine*, and so literally means 'to make manly'. That definition might feel a little too gender specific to our twenty-first-century ears, but there is an alternative.

Mettle has been used since the 1500s in English to refer to the inner strength or innermost makings of a person. Etymologically, it's nothing more than a variant spelling of *metal*, which first arrived in English as a general term for any solid metallic material in the thirteenth century. After the *mettle*-with-an-*le*-spelling established itself some three centuries later, for a time both it and the more usual *metal*-with-an-*al*-spelling were used interchangeably in English. But eventually, the two diverged: since the early 1700s onwards, we have tended to use *metal* for any solid metallic material, and *mettle* to refer figuratively to a person's inner strength.

It is this *mettle* that appears in expressions such as *test someone's mettle*, and *show your mettle*, both of which date from sometime around the sixteenth to seventeenth centuries. Though we don't tend to use it today, *to give mettle to someone* once likewise meant to encourage them, while *to be on your mettle* is to be motivated to try your best. *To put someone on their mettle* is to try their patience or resistance, and *to put someone off their mettle* is to undermine their confidence. Of all the *mettled* expressions the dictionary has to offer, however, one that is well worth bearing in mind here is *high-mettle* – a verb meaning 'to make courageous' or 'to invigorate'.

As an adjective, *high-mettled* has been used to mean 'showing great courage or resilience' since the early seventeenth century, and it was from this (now seldom encountered) expression that a verb, to *high-mettle*, was coined in the early 1800s. Whenever we feel our

courage failing, we need to *high-mettle* ourselves: summon up all the energy, valour and bravery we have, and
bolster ourselves into action.

See also: chalcentrous

HOWFFY

≈

*for when you're feeling uncomfortable
away from home*

Imagine having been delayed on a journey home, and being stuck in an uncomfortable, unfamiliar or uninviting place, tantalisingly close to your journey's end. There are quite a few soothing words of comfort and homeliness on which to focus your mind, while you wait to complete your trip home.

A *sonrock*, for instance, is a cosy fireside chair. A *hearthmuster* is a circle of friends and family gathered closely around a fireplace – as is an *ingle-ring*. To *cloff*, or *cluff*, is to relax by a fireside; to *crule* is to warm yourself in the light of a fire, and (perhaps most welcoming of all) an *ashypet*, or *ashiepattle*, is a household pet that likes to lounge next to the fire.

The fact that a lot of these words seem so concerned with the fireside is no coincidence and has great etymological significance. The Latin word for a central hearth or fireplace of a home was *focus*, and so central and important a location in the household did the hearthside prove that its name eventually came to be used of any central hub or 'focal' point.

To *leep*, likewise, is to snuggle or cosy up in a comfortable place. A *cherry-boose* is a snug and comfortable room. A *snoozing-crib* is a comfortable chair, as is a *lollockin* (derived from the verb *lollock*, meaning 'to lounge'). *Bachles* and *sleds* are old, worn-out shoes, comfortable enough to be worn as slippers, while *huffle-buffs* are worn-out, comfortable old clothes, and a *sheviton* is a worn-out, comfortable coat.

A *focillation* is a moment of comfort or refreshment. And, in eighteenth-century English at least, if you were feeling *picktooth*, then you were languishing and untroubled – literally, as if relaxing around a table, picking one's teeth after a hearty meal.

Of all the words for homeliness and home comforts, perhaps the most immediately appealing is an old dialect adjective, *howffy*. Derived from *howf*, or *hauff* – a word once found in several Scottish and northern English dialects for a much frequented haunt or a favourite pub – if you're feeling *howffy*, then you're snug and comfortable in a place you know well. Add a *hearthmuster* of your best and closest friends and family to that, and you can't go far wrong.

See also: angel-visits, antipelargy, heafgang

HURKLE-DURKLE

≈

*for when you have
the Monday-morning blues*

Your alarm goes off first thing on a Monday morning, and all you want to do is turn over in bed and go back to sleep. What you *don't* want to do is throw back the covers and ready yourself for a new week of work.

If it is any consolation, you're by no means alone in your hatred of Monday mornings, and there is quite a rich vocabulary of words and phrases to fall back on to describe precisely what you're up against. As well as being the name of the first day of the week, a *Monday* among British labourers was once a slangy nickname for an especially large sledgehammer, which, according to at least one dictionary definition, 'through the great exertion needed to wield it, brings you back to your senses when you return to work on Monday'.

To be *Mondayish* or *Mondayfied* in nineteenth-century English was to be disinclined to work, or to be especially tired and demotivated – 'a phrase that has its origin in the clergyman's supposed state of fatigue on Monday, after the work of Sunday', as *A Dictionary of Slang, Jargon and Cant* put it in 1889. Hangovers, likewise, were nicknamed *Monday-heads* by the Victorians, while *to keep Saint Monday* was a phrase apparently once used by cobblers who had returned to work after a heavy weekend:

> It is a custom . . . among shoemakers, if they intoxicate themselves on Sunday, to do no work on Monday; and this they call making a Saint Monday . . . Many have adopted this custom from the example of the shoemakers.
>
> Maria Edgeworth, *Popular Tales* (1804)

Whether nursing a *Monday-head* or not, the word you need for that lazy Monday-morning roll back into bed is *hurkle-durkle*, a term from the dialects of southern Scotland defined as 'to lie in bed, or to lounge after it is time to get up or go to work'.

That particular definition comes from John Jamieson's 1808 *Etymological Dictionary of the Scottish*

Language, which not only pinpointed the origin of the term to the county of Fife but suggested that it might have its origins in an old Germanic word, *durck*, or *durch*, for the hold of a ship. Perhaps Jamieson imagined some kind of etymological connection between someone lurking in the gloomy darkness beneath the covers of their bed, and someone lurking in the dim, musty store of a ship.

In so-called reduplicative or 'ricochet' words (built from two rhyming halves) such as these, it is often the case that the first part of the word acts as the original, motivating root, to which a second less meaningful part has been added as a little more than a sing-songy, humorous tag. In words such as *boogie-woogie*, *okey-dokey* and *lovey-dovey*, it's the root forms *boogie*, *okay* and *love* that bear the lion's share of the meaning. Far from alluding to the dank, dark hold of a ship then, it is more likely that *hurkle-durkle* is an extension of another old Scots word *hurkle*, or *hurkill*, meaning 'to draw the limbs together close to the body'. From there, it's easy to see where the image of someone cosily curled up in bed and reluctant to get up – not necessarily on a Monday morning – might ultimately have developed.

See also: frowst, self-soothe

INTERFULGENT

≈

for when you're feeling bleak or you lack hope

It never rains, but it pours. Or so people have been saying since the seventeenth century, when this old adage bemoaning the tendency of misfortunes to come in series was first recorded in the English language. It might be more than three hundred years old, but it's a saying that still rings true: when bad things happen, it often tends to feel as if they happen in succession, having the effect of knocking our confidence or spirit further back each time.

Having a trail of misfortunes in our personal lives is one thing, but in this fraught and fractious twenty-first century, all of these personal troubles can be compounded by the broader problems and worries we see affecting the world around us. The smaller our world has become over the years, the more amplified and immediate these global problems in it can appear. Before long, concerns about the state of the world, the environment, politics and all of the other troubles of the world can feel just as pressing to us as the problems we have in our day-to-day lives. Feeling powerless to do much about them ourselves, it can be difficult to have much hope for the future.

In seventeenth-century English, a person who had lost all hope was a *hopelost*. It's a word that has not stood the test of time (the *Oxford English Dictionary* has no record of it after the mid 1600s), but it's a feeling that will doubtless be familiar to many people. At its root is the word *hope* itself, which stands among the very earliest words in our language, having been unearthed in an Old English document dating from as far back as the ninth century. Back then, *hope* tended to be used to refer only to confidence or expectation in God, faith or religious salvation, but it wasn't long before the more general meaning we use today established itself in our vocabulary. People began *hoping for the best* in the fifteenth century, and *hoping against hope* in the nineteenth century. Oddly, the original *forlorn hope* was a party of troops or skirmishers, dispatched to the front line or front wave of a battle. Dating back to the mid 1500s, the words *forlorn hope* are actually a mangled version of an old Dutch expression, *'verloren hoop'* – literally, a 'lost troop'.

As bizarre etymological stories go, that which lies behind *forlorn hope* is one of the more surprising. But another (albeit more positive) phrase that is worth explaining here has an even more extraordinary tale attached to it.

In nineteenth-century slang (and, for that matter, still today in Australian and New Zealand English) having *Buckley's chance* or *Buckley's hope* was a proverbial expression for having absolutely no hope or chance of success at all. To say that there are just two chances of success, *Buckley's, or none*, means something is destined to fail, and there is little point in hoping otherwise. Ironically, however, these and a handful of other similar expressions all derive from an event of almost unbelievable success, and of triumph against the most extraordinarily slim of odds.

The *Buckley* in question here is William Buckley, an English soldier said to have been born in the tiny Cheshire village of Marton, near Macclesfield, in 1780. Around the turn of the century, Buckley was found guilty of possessing stolen goods in London and for his crime – as was the norm in the harsher justice system of the day – he was sentenced to be transported to Australia for a period of fourteen years.

Leaving England in 1803, Buckley arrived in Australia several months later, where he was tasked with helping to build a new settlement on a narrow spur of land on Port Phillip Bay, a vast inlet on which the city of Melbourne stands today. This new settlement was soon plagued with a multitude of problems, notably a lack of nearby fresh water, and so it was eventually decided to abandon the site and relocate the entire settlement off the mainland, on Van Diemen's Land (modern-day Tasmania).

It was in the lead-up to this relocation that Buckley and a band of his fellow convicts took the opportunity to flee. According to at least one account of their escape, under cover of darkness they stole a rowing boat, sailed back across Port Phillip Bay to the mainland, and disappeared into the bush. What happened to Buckley's accomplices is unknown; some reports claimed at least one man was shot and killed during the escape, while another suggests that the men instantly separated as soon as they reached the other side of the bay and never saw one another again. A search was launched to recapture the men, but after several weeks it was presumed that all of them had perished in the unforgiving Australian outback. In fact, Buckley had had an extraordinary stroke of luck.

Having fended for himself in the bush for several days (or weeks, or even months, depending on which account you believe), Buckley stumbled across a group of Aboriginal women, who were members of the local Wadawurrung people. They quickly befriended him, and seeing that he was in need of sustenance, took him back with them to their nearby camp.

The women's instantaneous hospitableness, some versions of the story claim, was due to Buckley reportedly approaching them holding a spear he had found stabbed into the ground nearby, which the Wadawurrung had used to mark the grave of one of their relatives who had recently died. Recognising the spear in his hand, the women presumed Buckley to be the spirit of their deceased friend, and consequently ushered him all but immediately back to their camp. Whether or not that is the real story of how Buckley first encountered the Wadawurrung, remarkably, he went on to live with them for the next thirty-two years.

After all that time, news finally reached Buckley that a ship had been spotted anchored off the coast of the Bellarine Peninsula, south west of Melbourne, and that a new encampment of settlers had arrived on the mainland. In July 1835, he wandered into the camp and revealed his identity, to the astonishment of all those living there. Two months later – and eighteen years after his original sentence would have been completed – he was granted a pardon by Sir George Arthur, Lieutenant-General of Van Diemen's Land.

How much of William Buckley's story is true and how much of it is later exaggeration and legend does not matter. It is his miraculous escape – and his even more miraculous survival, against all odds, in the Australian outback – that lies at the origin of the expression *Buckley's chance*. Odd, then, that a phrase meaning 'no hope' or 'no likelihood', *Buckley's chance*, should have its origins in a tale proving that there is always hope, always an outside chance, and, despite the odds stacked against you, always some likelihood of success.

Buckley's story is one that inspires us to remain positive even when faced with the very slimmest of odds. But what about a word for remaining positive not just in the face of unlikelihood or improbability, but when struggling through difficult, bleak and troubling times? In a dark world, we need a word that brings in the light. In short, we need something *interfulgent*.

The adjective *interfulgent* describes anything that shines through or between something else – like dappled beams of sunlight breaking through the leaves and boughs of trees. It is a beautiful, useful and inspirational word – yet also a criminally underused one, seldom recorded in the language since it first emerged in the early eighteenth century.

Etymologically, it brings together two Latin roots: *inter*, meaning 'between', and *fulgere*, a Latin verb meaning 'to shine' or 'gleam'. That same verb is found at the root of a host of equally illuminating words, like *refulgence* and *effulgence*, both meaning 'radiance' or 'brilliance'; *fulgur*, a sixteenth-century word for a single flash of lightning, and *prefulgent*, an adjective meaning 'outshining' or, by extension, 'outperforming'. Admittedly, any one of these words could be taken as a reminder that, even in dark times, there is always light. But uniquely *interfulgent* reinforces that fact by implying that light always manages to shine through whatever tries to obscure it. Times may be dark at the moment, certainly, but there could well be light at the end of the tunnel – or, for that matter, on the other side of the trees.

See also: agathism, eucatastrophe, meliorism

KENGOOD

≈

for when you're dealing with regret

The French expression *esprit de l'escalier* is one of the more useful phrases the English language has adopted from another language. Often translated as simply 'staircase wit', *esprit de l'escalier* refers to the excruciating phenomenon of thinking of the perfect remark or witty rejoinder only long after the time to drop our ideal *bon mot* into conversation has passed. According to etymological legend, the phrase was inspired by (though not coined by) the eighteenth-century philosopher and writer Denis Diderot, who, while visiting the home of the French statesman Jacques Necker (a government minister in the court of Louis XVI), was caught off guard by a barbed remark and struggled to come up with an appropriate reply. 'A sensible man such as myself,' he later wrote, 'when overwhelmed by an argument levelled against him, becomes confused and can only think clearly again at the bottom of the stairs.'

Given how eminently useful an expression it is, it's perhaps unsurprising that *esprit de l'escalier* has long since found its way into English and has been in independent use in the language for over a century. The fact that we use the original French phrase to describe this phenomenon, however, has led to *esprit de l'escalier* mistakenly being touted as an example of yet another foreign expression of which the English language has no native equivalent. In fact, when it comes to thinking up or realising things too late, English has quite a stout vocabulary.

To remember something with a pang of regret, for instance, is to *remord* it. Knowledge or wisdom that is accrued too late to have been of any use has been known as *afterwit*, *after-light* and *latter-wit* since the mid 1500s; the opposite is *forewit*, while a *man-of-after-wits* was, in seventeenth-century English, a man who always professed to be an expert only after mistakes had been made.

An *after-thinker* is someone who acts first, only to go on to consider the effects of their actions (usually with regret) later. Someone described as *Epimethean* – a reference to the Ancient Greek demigod Epimetheus, twin brother of the considerably better-known Prometheus

– similarly tends to act without thinking of the consequences. According to legend, Epimetheus was given the task of doling out talents and traits among the animals of the world, but by the time he reached mankind he had run out of traits to distribute. His lack of foresight ultimately led to his brother, Prometheus, stealing fire from the gods and giving it to mankind instead.

Of all the words the dictionary has to offer when it comes to regretting our actions, however, perhaps one of the most peculiar is *hadiwist*. *Wis* is an archaic word meaning 'to know' – and so 'had I wist' essentially means 'would that I had known'. Given that etymology, it is likely that *hadiwist* first emerged in the language as a doleful cry or exclamation of regret, called out when a mistake or missed opportunity is first realised. From the fourteenth century onwards, however, *hadiwist* has been used as a noun rather than an expression: as one *Dictionary of Early English* defines it, a *hadiwist* is 'a vain regret' or 'the heedlessness that results in it'.

It is only natural to make mistakes and to regret them. The trick is to put a positive spin on these errors, missteps and wasted opportunities. To help us on our way to doing that, there is the word *kengood*.

Like the 'wis' of *hadiwist*, the 'ken' of *kengood*, or *kenguid*, is another word meaning 'to know' or 'to be aware of'.

Attached to the standard English word *good*, *kengood* essentially means 'to know well' or 'to pay close attention to' – or, as at least one dictionary definition puts it, a *kengood* is 'a warning', 'a caveat' or, most importantly here, 'a lesson got by experience'. So we might make errors and regret them, and we might miss opportunities and lament letting them pass us by, but the word *kengood* reminds us that we can always learn never to make the same mistakes again. Live by that rule, and every bad experience or regrettable decision becomes an opportunity for improvement, education and growth, and the less likely we are to fall foul of *esprit de l'escalier*.

See also: armogan, to pipe in an ivy leaf

MELIORISM

≋

*for when you're worried about
the future of the world*

Being worried about the direction in which the world has been heading so far in the twenty-first century doesn't necessarily make you a pessimist. It might even make you a realist.

It's fair to say that the world has faced its fair share of problems in recent years, and not all of them have yet been solved or handled justly – and indeed a fair few of them might yet get worse before they get any better. The pessimist would have you believe that the world has already gone awry and that it is too late to do anything; the optimist would blindly tell you that all the world's problems will sort themselves out in the end, no problem at all; the AGATHIST realises that yes, the world faces many challenges, but believes that there is still time to do something about them and for all things to eventually improve. This is our more realist thinker, but the *agathist* is, in essence, content to let things improve around them. What about someone more proactive? A thinker who looks at the world around them as it is today (and, more importantly, who looks ahead to a world that is now beginning to take shape) and wants to improve matters. For that, perhaps we need a different way of thinking – and a word no less reassuring, but somewhat more inspiring.

Meliorism is the belief that the world, no matter what shape it might be in, can always be improved by the concerted effort of mankind. As an outlook on life, it was popularised by the Victorian philosopher and psychologist James Sully in an 1877 work entitled (somewhat ironically) *Pessimism*. But far from coining the term himself, in his work Sully credited *meliorism* to someone he had had the pleasure of meeting, interviewing and eventually befriending while researching for the book. *Meliorism*, Sully explained, was the work of the English novelist George Eliot.

In their conversations together, Eliot had seemingly touched on her own personal outlook on life, and mentioned that she had given it the name *meliorism* – a term derived from *melior*, a Latin word meaning 'better' or 'stronger', which unsurprisingly makes it an etymological cousin of words including *ameliorate* and *melioration*, the act of improving or bettering something. 'She herself', Sully later recounted of their time together, 'held a view midway between those of the optimist and the pessimist, to which she gave the name of meliorism.' When it came to putting together his work on the subject, Sully asked Eliot if he could credit the word to her in his work, but it seems she was initially somewhat hesitant. 'I don't know that I ever heard anybody use the world "meliorist" except myself,' she wrote in letter to him in 1877. 'But I begin to think that there is no good invention or discovery that has not been made by more than one person.' With that caveat in mind, she gave Sully permission to use her name but, in typically self-effacing fashion, only if he 'found it useful for the doctrine of meliorism to cite one unfashionable confessor of it' as a means of thinking. Eliot's letter now provides the earliest written record of the word *meliorism* of which we know.

Sully's writings (doubtless along with the cachet of using a word invented by one of the era's most acclaimed authors) helped popularise *meliorism* among Victorian thinkers and philosophers. Over time, they seemingly broadened and built on Eliot's original concept, so that far from being merely operating as a 'midway' view between optimism and pessimism, *meliorism* became something of a pragmatic call to arms – a belief that a better world is not only possible but inarguably worth taking the effort to create.

See also: agathism, eucatastroph, interfulgent, traumatropism, the worse the passage, the more welcome the port

MINDING

≈

for when you miss someone

'Solitary, from some person or thing being a-missing or absent.' That's how an 1802 explanatory glossary of Scots poetry defined the tragically useful word *misslie*. If you're feeling *misslie*, then you're dearly missing something or someone from your life.

This will doubtless be a familiar feeling to anyone who has endured grief or loss, or has seen a close friend or relative move away from home and take their much missed warmth and friendship – and their everyday place in your life – with them. Mourning the loss of someone who has died is very different from missing someone who is simply not as close at hand as they once were. For that reason, these vastly different circumstances are dealt with under separate words: the memorialising MONTH'S-MIND is there for remembering someone after they have died; STOUND to remind you that you aren't suffering alone; DRUERY if you're mourning the end of a relationship; and HOWFFY, HEAFGANG and ANGEL-VISITS for missing home or familiar faces. But for the general, somewhat discomforting feeling of missing someone close – for whatever reason – we need something a little different. We need, one way or another, a *reminder*.

At the root of the word *reminder* is the word *mind*. One of the barest bare bones of the English language, *mind* has been used of a person's mental faculty or intellect since the early Old English period, with one of its earliest recorded uses having been discovered in a document dating from sometime in the eighth century. In all of its earliest Old English contexts, however, *mind* referred specifically to memory, and the brain's ability to recall, recollect and remember. *Mind* has long since expanded into a more general term for all of the brain's cognitive processes, but this age-old sense of the word can still be found in stock expressions such as *to call to mind* and *to bear in mind*, and at the root of related words, such as *remind* and *reminder*.

In some dialects of English, this ancient use of *mind* to refer specifically to memory survived, with a number of regional English dictionaries listing *mind* as a verb essentially meaning 'to recall' or, conversely, 'to be prompted to recollect'. Derived from that, a *mind-ing* is an instance of recollection or a single memory; a forgotten thought cast back into your consciousness, or a memento or token, serving to remind someone of something, and keep them from forgetting it. And it is this *minding* that concerns us here.

When someone is no longer in our lives, the things that we now have that were once theirs suddenly become so much more meaningful. These keepsakes can of course already be hugely meaningful in themselves – but, in truth, that need not necessarily be the case. For every treasured photograph, there is a handwritten note scribbled in the margin of a book. For every antique wedding ring, there is a door key, a car key, a pair of spectacles, a favourite cup or pen. Everyday objects that the person we are missing knew, and liked, and used are all but transformed into precious heirlooms when their owner is no longer in our lives. They might mean little to anybody else, and taken out of context might carry no importance whatsoever, but to us and to anyone aware of their import and heritage, they carry a tanta-lising connection to a much loved person that we can simply no longer see.

These *mindings*, as we can now call them, can be upsetting, especially when our sense of loss is still quite new. But they can also be immensely comforting and reassuring, giving us a tangible, tactile connection to the people that we miss, complementing our thoughts and memories of them. They can *remind* us of the people we once had in our lives in more ways than one.

See also: angel-visits, antipelargy, druery, heafgang, month's-mind, stound

MONTH'S-MIND

≋

for when you're in mourning

Losing someone we care deeply about is an upsetting and profoundly life-altering event. The shock and grief of the initial loss can be agonising and debilitating, but the grieving process is a long one, and as the days and weeks go by, that initial grief eventually begins to fade. But even as we work to rebuild our lives – and for that matter, even after we have rebuilt them – we still continue to mourn. Arguably, mourning someone we have lost is a process that never ceases, as every time we think of them and miss having them in our lives, we mourn for their loss – and it's likely that we always will.

It might be tempting to shy away from thinking of whoever it is we have lost in order not to upset ourselves. But if we consider that the pain of mourning someone is a testament to how much they meant to us, then keeping them in our thoughts seems much more bearable. And as painful as it might be, thinking of those you have lost is a welcome and comforting way of keeping them in your life after they have gone. A *month's-mind* is a word for precisely these times: it is a commemorative celebration held precisely one month after a much loved person has passed away.

In Scots, Irish and other Celtic regions' cultures in particular, there is a long-held tradition of observing this *month's-mind* or one-month anniversary, with written accounts of such celebrations dating back as far as the fifteenth century, though the tradition itself is doubtless considerably older. In other cultures, however, this kind of celebration is not so frequently observed – though the thinking behind it might well be something familiar to anyone who has suffered a bereavement.

In the time after a loss, the anniversaries of that loss become landmarks in the calendar, as first the days, then weeks, months and finally years without that person in our lives begin to mount up. We might not see these landmarks as 'celebrations', nor will we always look to observe them overtly or publicly, but they will no doubt seem significant to us as we continue the process of living with a loss. Regardless of whether we see a *month's-mind* as a public celebration or as a private observation, the word itself is a reassuring reminder that grief is a process built around taking each day as it comes – but never forgetting those who are no longer here to share those days with.

See also: minding, stound

MOOREEFFOC

≋

*for when you're losing interest
or lacking inspiration*

An 1862 guide to the *Dialect of Leeds* included among its entries the word *maungy*, an adjective defined as 'ill-tempered and peevish', like a 'spoiled child . . . [who] refuses to take pleasure in what generally affords it a great deal'. A related verb, *maunge*, can be variously used to mean 'to sulk', 'to be dissatisfied' or 'to move or act listlessly'. So when you're bored, tired or annoyed, and even settling down to your favourite book or pastime fails to improve your mood, then you're feeling *maungy*.

Like a lot of dialect words, the etymological origins of *maunge* and *maungy* are difficult to pin down. But with its clear associations with irritability and restlessness, it is probably a somewhat distant relative of *mangy*, which has been used in a figurative sense – to mean 'shabby', 'mean' or 'distasteful' – for almost as long as it has been used in English at all.

Everyone goes through a bit of *maunginess* every now and then, when even the things we enjoy just don't seem to cut it for us any more. It could be tiredness, stress, frustration, boredom or any one of a range of feelings and emotions that sparks this sluggish ennui, and it can take a real shake-up of our routine to snap us out of it.

But if you're just generally becoming bored with the everyday things around you – and, in particular, with the things that normally keep you happy and moti-vated – then perhaps you merely need to shake up your perspective, and be inspired to see the world around you with new eyes. For that, we have one of the most unusual words in this collection – and an etymological tale that takes us back to the shabby coffee houses of Victorian London.

In the late 1840s, Charles Dickens began writing his autobiography. Countless notes and anecdotes were sketched, but Dickens never saw the project through to fruition and instead, in 1849, handed all these miscel-laneous autobiographical notes over to his longstanding friend John Forster, who had recently taken over as the editor of Dickens' periodical, *The Daily News*. After Dickens' death in 1870, Forster took it on himself to complete his friend's life story for him, and, after many months' work, published the first volume of his grand *Life of Charles Dickens* in 1872. In it, Forster included a brief and seemingly inconsequential story Dickens had noted down about his childhood in London:

> When I had money enough, I used to go to a coffee-shop and have half-a-pint of coffee and a slice of bread and butter . . . The coffee-shops to which I most resorted were one in Maiden-lane, one in a court (non-existent now) close to Hungerford-market, and one in St Martin's-lane, of which I only recollect that it stood near the church, and that in the door there was an oval glass-plate, with COFFEE-ROOM painted on it, addressed towards the street. If I ever find myself in a very different kind of coffee-room now, but where there is such an inscription on the glass, and read it backward on the wrong side MOOR-EEFFOC (as I often used to then, in a dismal reverie), a shock goes through my blood.

The word *mooreeffoc* is simply a reversal of the words 'coffee room', which Dickens as a child had glimpsed through the glass of a coffee-house door. For Dickens himself, this word offered little more than a chance reminiscence of his youth every time he saw the same mirrored letters in his adulthood. But to another of his biographers, it meant something quite different.

In 1906, G. K. Chesterton wrote his own biographical appraisal of Dickens and included in it the story of the *mooreeffoc* as an example of the endless fertility of Dickens' imagination. 'Dickens could always vitalise some dark or dull corner of London,' he wrote. 'There are details in the Dickens descriptions . . . which he endows with demoniac life.' *Mooreeffoc*, Chesteron wrote, was a 'wild word' that exemplifies 'the principle that the most fantastic thing of all is often the precise fact'. Dickens' gift as an almost impossibly imaginative writer was to see all these everyday 'facts' through new eyes, transforming them into wild new things that had never been seen or conceived of before.

Not everyone can profess to being as inspired and inventive a thinker as Dickens but his casual observance of a reversed coffee-house sign all those years ago has given us a word for following in his imaginative footsteps. When we become bored by the everyday world and all the sights and sounds in it, taking a step back and appraising it with a fresh pair of eyes can be all that is needed to revitalise our thinking, gain a better understanding of it and revive our interest or approach to it.

Precisely what it is that you need to apply this *mooreeffoc* approach to is up to you: it could be a book you've struggled to finish, a hobby that has fallen by the wayside or just a dreary boredom with the same old streets. What *mooreeffoc* proves is that things don't in themselves become boring but that we allow ourselves to become bored with them. Change that way of thinking, and we can change the world around us.

See also: aganippe, autoschediasm

NUGIFRIVOLOUS

≋

*for when you're obsessing
over unimportant things*

Life can be challenging enough at times without over-loading our minds and mental to-do lists with tasks and unimportant trivialities that, although will probably have to be dealt with at some point in the future, are not in need of being tackled right away.

The more level-headed and laidback among us don't face this problem; free time is precious, so why fill it with things that, in the grand scheme of things, really don't matter? But those of us who delight in keeping ourselves busy, and who see jobs that need doing even where there are none, are more susceptible to this manic busyness. Here are the people who clean out the spare room, only to end up noticing the skirting boards need repainting while they're at it. Here are people who agree to have relatives over to stay, only to end up cleaning the oven and tidying the loft. And here are people who go searching for a favourite book, only to end up alphabetising their entire bookcase to make any future hunt somewhat less time consuming.

If all of this sounds familiar, and you're aware that you're the kind of person who finds jobs even where there are none, then you can console yourself with the fact that there is at least a word for your state of mind. Dating from the late eighteenth century, *nugaemania* is an obsession with trifling issues – which makes someone who obsesses over unimportant jobs a *nugaemaniac*.

Nugae was a Latin word for jokes, japes and other nonsensical trivialities, and it is from there that this pair of eminently useful words has derived, alongside a host of similarly throwaway concerns. Something that is *nugatory* is of little real value. A *nugament* is an unimportant object or task. And English has even adopted a Latin stock expression, *nugae difficiles* – literally 'difficult trifles' – to describe what the *Oxford English Dictionary* astutely defines as 'difficult but trivial matters, over which a disproportionate amount of time may be taken'. *Nugae difficiles*, then, is essentially an impressively classical reminder that we shouldn't sweat the small stuff.

Being the kind of person who keeps themselves constantly busy is by no means a bad thing, of course. But when you're busying yourself with things that can hardly be described as important, then perhaps we need a word to help keep matters in proportion.

Tasks that don't need doing right away, for instance, can be *perendinated* – that is, put off for a couple of days. Derived from the Latin *dies perendinus*, meaning 'the day after tomorrow', the verb *perendinate* has long since fallen out of use since first appearing in the language in the 1600s (although it is arguably in need of a revival). An even earlier word, *resplait*, means 'to delay something until after further consideration'. Dating back as far as the 1400s in English, *resplait* fell out of use in the sixteenth century in all contexts except for Scottish law, where it remained for a time a word for adjourning or deferring the judgement of a case until a future date. And to *fode*, in Tudor-period English, was to deceive or lead on someone with flatteringly kind words. Derived from that usage, an expression *to fode forward*, or *to fode off*, developed in the sixteenth century, meaning 'to put off doing something by inventing evasive excuses'. If you really can't be bothered to busy yourself with the tasks at hand, try convincing yourself *why* you shouldn't do them.

If you're a habitual *nugaemaniac*, however, then perhaps the best word for you is an etymological relative
that also happens to be its direct opposite. Coined as
far back as 1589, if you're *nugifrivolous*, then you have
enough free time to devote to pointless frivolities.

Essentially, *nugifrivolous* is a word to persuade you
that when, at long last, some well-earned free time
finally arrives in your calendar, the last thing you should
do is spend it filling your day with tasks and problems
that don't need addressing immediately – or, for that
matter, do not warrant addressing at all. If you have
the time spare to invent chores and jobs to satiate the
nugaemaniac in you, then you surely have time to please
the *nugifrivolous* part of you too, and fill your day with all
of the frivolous hobbies and fun you can think of. You
might just need to take a step back to be able to see it.

OPSIMATHY

≈

for when you're feeling held back by age

One of the more alarming aspects of growing old is the feeling that age is now a barrier for doing what you want to do, and that past opportunities have been missed.

German being the endlessly inventive language that it is, it can be relied on for the perfect word for the feeling that time is running short. *Torschlusspanik* is often defined as simply the German equivalent of a midlife crisis but bundled up in that extraordinary mouthful of a word is considerably more than that. *Torschlusspanik* encapsulates a feeling that your opportunities and chances in life are now passing you by, that the time to act on them has either gone by already or is fast approaching, and that, as a result, you'll be compelled to act more rashly, or with a less considered approach in the future, in order not to run out of time completely.

Torschlusspanik literally means 'gate-closing panic', and etymological folklore would have you believe its origins lie back in the days of the walled and heavily fortified towns and cities of medieval Europe. Supposedly anyone straying outside the walls of the city too long or too late at night would risk a race against time to return home before the city gates were locked for the evening, and *Torschlusspanik* is popularly said to have been invented to describe this last-minute dash home to avoid a night out in the wilds. The word is likely to be a much more modern invention than that story might suggest – but that's not to say that it's any less useful or evocative a word.

To counteract this breathless race against time, and to give us some much needed reassurance that there is always time left on the clock, are a group of words that remind us that it is never too late to do anything. Among them is *opsimathy*, a term coined in the mid seventeenth century for beginning to study – or else returning to study or education – later in life. Someone who does precisely that is an *opsimath*.

The 'math' in words like *opsimathy* and *opsimath* is also found in words such as *mathematics* and *polymath*. It comes to us from a Greek word meaning 'lesson' or, literally, 'that which is learned'. The prefix *opsi-* comes from the Greek word for 'late', *opse*, and is found in English in another age-defying word, *opsigamy* – a nineteenth-century invention meaning 'a marriage undertaken late in life'.

Opsimathy itself was originally somewhat frowned on as a failing or defect and was not viewed as being particularly positive or advisable when the word first appeared in the language in the seventeenth century. 'Old men are very unfit learners of the lessons which the world teacheth,' wrote the English theologian John Hales in 1656, 'and almost impossible it is for a man to begin to study in his age.' *Opsimathy*, he continued, is 'a great vice' and considered 'very unseemly among moral and natural men'. Thankfully, those times changed.

By the 1800s, the practice of learning late in life was beginning to be seen more as something to be encouraged – a change in viewpoint perhaps driven in part by the number of leading figures in the Victorian era who, driven to better themselves and the world around them during the Industrial Revolution, excelled despite a humble start in life or a poor childhood education. The earlier stigma that studying in later life once had (along with many of the other conventions and customs of earlier times) began to be challenged and rethought in the nineteenth century, and that process has continued ever since. Today, returning to or beginning education in later life is not only encouraged but often applauded.

As such, *opsimathy* is a word that demonstrates that, no matter what your age might be, there is always time left on the clock, and that time can always be used to your advantage. Ageing may close some doors but certainly not all of them. The key remains, as always, to merely make the most of all the time we have left.

See also: beauté du diable, carpe noctem, worldcraft

TO PIPE IN AN IVY LEAF

≋

for when you feel like a failure

Nike (as in the sportswear brand) is the name of the Greek goddess of victory. *Hedone* (as in the word *hedonism*) was a Greek word for pleasure. Put those two concepts together, and you have *nikhedonia*, a term from psychology for the sweet, adrenalin-raising excitement of anticipating success.

Whether that success ever materialises or not is another matter. We have already (under ALLABORATE) met the daydreaming market trader Alnaschar, and his subsequent daydream-bursting brush with *Alnascharism* and *anticipointment*. Just like Alnaschar's doomed path to great wealth and power, not every action or idea we plan out will lead to success, and dealing with, learning from and ultimately recovering after a crushing failure is one of life's most important, if least welcome, lessons.

The sheer number of words and phrases the dictionary has to describe failures and fiascos at least offers some consolation that in not seeing your ideas come to fruition successfully, you are by no means alone. In nineteenth-century slang, a crushing failure was a *bloomer*, a *dimracker* or a *dead frost*. Proverbially, *to bring your eggs to a bad market* (or, oddly, *to bring your pigs to a fine market*) has meant to be unsuccessful in some attempted venture since the mid 1600s. And while a *purler* is a thumping, knockout blow, *to come a purler* is to suffer an equally resounding defeat.

Anyone who fails in an undertaking can at least console themselves that they tried. This sentiment, and the gamble that anyone risking some grand enterprise takes, is neatly summed up in the nineteenth-century expression *to make a spoon, or spoil a horn*. As one contemporary dictionary helpfully explains, this phrase alludes to 'a man who wants to carve a spoon out of a cow's horn', which 'a bungling craftsman would be sure to make sad work of'. In other words, the craftsman will either succeed in his undertaking, or ruin his work beyond repair – but either way, at least he took the chance. After all, the fear of trying something and then failing can be even more damaging than the failure itself, and can lead to a lifetime of missed opportunities and chances never taken.

In psychology, the fear of failure is properly known as *kakorrhaphiophobia*, a term imaginatively derived at length from Greek words meaning 'bad' and 'sewing seeds'. Holding back from attempting something out of the fear of failing is also known as the *Jonah complex* – an allusive reference to the biblical prophet Jonah, who initially fled when approached by God to carry out his work. Jonah's longstanding reputation as a doubter, a pessimist and a naysayer has long since become immortalised in the language too: as a verb, to *jonah* is to appear to doom whatever you involve yourself in with failure, or to ruin whatever you attempt to do.

Take heart in your failure that you are not a Jonah: you have, at least, attempted something, regardless of its outcome. In failure, there are always lessons to be learned (as the handsome word KENGOOD tells us). But failures can nevertheless still be demoralising and, depending on their extent, they can prove difficult to process and shake off. In order to help things along, why not *pipe in an ivy leaf*?

This peculiar expression is an ancient one. Geoffrey Chaucer used it several times in his writing back in the 1300s, and an even earlier incarnation has since been unearthed in an Anglo-Saxon text dating from more than three centuries before him. Its origins are admittedly somewhat mysterious. The *ivy-leaf* has long been used as a symbol for anything fairly trivial and throwaway, probably a nod to how common and how easy to cultivate ivy bushes are, while *pipe* in this instance is a verb, meaning 'to blow down' or 'to whistle into', as if playing a musical instrument. It has been suggested that an *ivy-leaf* might once have been some kind of frivolous child's toy – perhaps a rudimentary wooden flute or whistle. But no matter the precise image or meaning behind it, *to pipe in* or *with an ivy-leaf* means to engage in some pointless, light-hearted activity, of little or no consequence to anything – especially if, in doing so, you are consoling yourself after a bruising failure.

While expressions such as the *Jonah complex* tell us to take heart in the fact that we at least tried while other people might have held back, *to pipe in an ivy-leaf* reminds us of the importance of being kind to ourselves in the aftermath of a failure. While we regroup and learn from our mistakes, taking some much needed time off, doing nothing but indulging in something that we simply enjoy or that pleases us, and has no meaningful consequences attached to it is a fine way to help to rebuild our confidence and soothe our bruised spirits.

See also: kengood

PSAPHONISE

≋

for when life seems to lack reward or purpose

Some people are supreme self-motivators. Whatever they turn their mind or skills to, they do so with great energy and enthusiasm, and simply enjoy the process of doing it without any thought of reward or goal. Other people, however, are less driven. Without the promise of a reason or reward for doing something, they simply drift listlessly and without focus, and end up embarking on whatever task they have before them so grudgingly that they doom themselves to failure almost before they have begun. Even worse than that, this lack of a meaningful goal or objective might prove so demoralising that they end up not actually *doing* anything at all.

Supremely energetic self-motivators are said to be *autotelic* people. A term used in fields such as psychology and theology, an *autotelic* person is someone who enjoys the participation or performance of something more than they would any eventual reward or objective. The opposite is a *heterotelic* person – someone who requires there to be some greater purpose or goal in place in order to work or achieve to the best of their ability. Both of these terms derive from a Greek word for an end or goal, *telos*, which is also found at the root of such brilliant words as *telesiurgic* ('capable of accomplishing a desired goal') and *telesis* ('effort or intellectual direction towards an objective'). Oddly, it is also the origin of the word *talisman*, as the ancient ceremonies at which these magical charms and amulets would once have been used were typically carried out with some eventual purpose, or *telos*, in mind.

If you are an *autotelic* person, then you need little help here: you are your own motivation and motivator, and the enjoyment you get out of merely attempting or completing something is enough of a reward for you. If you're more of a *heterotelic* person, then not having a goal in mind can prove unhelpful. Without a path or purpose, one day can merge into the next, and before long you might have let far too much time and opportunity pass you by. We need a word, then, to help get things back on track. And it just so happens that it's one of the most peculiar words on this list.

In 1836, an essay appeared in *American Monthly*, a journal dedicated to discussions of literature and the arts founded by the English-born author and scholar Henry William Herbert. The author of the essay (who remained anonymous) bemoaned both a growing lack of imagination among English speakers to build and adopt new words, and the closed-mindedness of language purists, who shunned words adopted from other languages. To support the argument, the author coined a series of new words – *psaphonism*, *psaphonise*, *psaphonific* – based on a bizarre tale from the ancient world.

According to legend, Psapho, or Psaphon, was a humble man in Ancient Libya, who wished above all else to achieve great fame and wealth, and to wield great influence. In order to achieve his goal, he decided he needed to make his name known among the people of Libya, and so he tamed a vast flock of mimicking birds and trained them to parrot, 'Psapho is a god.' He then set the birds free, and as they flew off across the surrounding country, they took Psapho's self-aggrandising message with them as they went. His plan was an extraordinary success: the local people eventually accepted his name into their pantheon of gods, and when he finally made his identity known, Psapho was instantly adopted by the people as their king.

The author goes on to argue that this kind of boastful self-promotion should be known as *psaphonism* in Psapho's honour, that the act of 'schooling, bribing' and otherwise influencing the opinions of the people in this way should be described as *psaphonific*, and that Psaphon's name should likewise be immortalised in a related verb, to *psaphonise*, meaning 'to puff one's self in one's own newspaper'. (Despite writing almost two centuries ago, the author also, somewhat presciently, went so far as to draw parallels with the role of the press in political elections: 'Now if anyone will diligently study all our newspapers, he will find about election seasons something in them analogous to the voices of Psaphon's birds.')

Unfortunately, none of these words has ever gained much traction, but on the rare occasions that allusive references to Psapho do appear, they tend not to be used in reference to self-aggrandisement and bluster, but to Psapho's determined attempt to achieve his goal, no matter how grand or ludicrous a scheme he would have to adopt. A *psaphonic* plan is one built around achieving great success. *Psaphonism* is goal-driven, relentlessly ambitious behaviour. And to *psaphonise* is to plot your path to fame and fortune.

Your personal goal might not be quite so ambitious as Psapho's zeal for godlike influence but if you're the kind of person who struggles to motivate themselves without a clear path or objective ahead of you, then Psapho's tale – and the word *psaphonise* itself – is a wise reminder that it is always worth taking time to figure out what you wish to achieve, and how best you might be able to achieve it.

See also: aganippe

REDAMANCY

~

for when your love is unrequited

At some point in their lives, virtually everyone will fall for someone they know they cannot have, or who does not return their affection as readily as they might have hoped. And as anyone who has navigated such unrequited love will doubtless know, turning off those feelings and silencing the voice in your head telling you to think about your latest infatuation is considerably more easily said than done.

When we're deep in the midst of a romantic predicament like this, our minds can easily become fogged and muddled, as we end up dealing with not only the anguish of our unreciprocated feelings but a crisis of confidence too. You might begin to feel as though you'll never find anyone else. You might feel as if you're now destined to be alone forever. And in an endless search to resolve the situation, you might start wondering what it is that's wrong with you, why that person couldn't love you back. The hard truth of the matter is simple, however: sometimes, these things just aren't meant to be.

The language of unrequited love contains many choice words and emotions. A *swellack* is someone whose self-esteem has been extinguished. *Aphilophrenia* is the feeling that you are unloved. *Eremophobia* is the fear of loneliness, or the fear that you will never find another partner. A *desiderium* is a feeling of longing for something that you have lost or cannot have. In Old English, *sorhlufu* was love mingled with feelings of woe and anxiety; despite its usefulness, no one has used that word for a thousand years. And to *alamort* is to pine with loneliness or dejection; somewhat unnervingly, it is a compounding of the French phrase *à la mort*, literally 'to the death'.

The word for what we're searching for in all of this melancholy is *redamancy*, or *redamation*. Coined in the seventeenth century, *redamancy* is a word defined by one dictionary as early as 1656 as 'a loving of him or her that loves us'. In other words, *redamancy* is reciprocated, mutual love.

Redamancy might seem like a distant or unlikely prospect when we're in the throes of pulling ourselves through a failed or unrequited relationship, but the fact that the word even exists in our language (and that it has endured in the dictionary for four centuries) should give us comfort. After all, just because this one romance has failed to come to fruition, does not mean that *redamancy* itself has ceased to be a prospect. There will always be another future object of our desire who *will* return our affections, and who will bring some much longed-for *redamancy* into our lives. The only challenge then is in finding that person. But, alas, the dictionary can't quite help us with that . . .

See also: anacampserote, druery

RESPAIR

≈

for when you're in despair

English picked up the word *despair* from French sometime around the early fourteenth century. Etymologically, at its root is the Latin verb *sperare*, meaning 'to hope', but the prefix *de-* works to undo or reverse that core meaning – so that *despair* literally describes a total absence of hope.

A world without hope is an almost unbearable thought. But when times prove unkind, or when one problem so swiftly follows another that we feel overwhelmed by difficulties, despair can be a very real feeling. What it takes to help us out of that hopelessness depends very much on what appears to be at the root of it: CULTELLATION, for instance, can help with a feeling of being deluged by problems; INTERFULGENT works to provide a literal glimmer of hope in a bleak time; and both AGATHISM and MELIORISM give a more realistic and forward-thinking spin on a pessimistic, dejected outlook on life.

If you're despairing about the state of the wider world, it might help to know that there are words like *omniparity* ('universal fairness'), *panpolism* ('absolute equality of civil rights'), *adequation* ('the act of making all things equal'), *dicaearch* ('a thoroughly just and fair leader') and *isocracy* ('a government in which everyone possesses equal power'). If you're despairing about your place in the world, how about *vitativeness* ('a desire to live'), or *biophilia* ('a love of life and all living things'). Or if you're pained by the way we seem to treat one another, there are always words such as *neiperty* ('neighbourliness', 'community spiritedness'), and *confelicity* ('happiness in seeing other people happy') with which to lighten your spirits.

Given that the word *despair* itself has 'hope' at its etymological centre, ironically perhaps the one word we need here is all but directly in front of us.

First used sometime in the mid 1400s, *respair* is fresh or reinvigorated hope, while as a verb to *respair* means 'to recover or have renewed hope'. Tellingly, the word *respair* has never much caught on in the language, and records of its use in the time since its earliest appearance in the fifteenth century have proved difficult to unearth. As a result, *respair* sits on the sidelines of the language along with a handful of other long-overlooked and long-forgotten opposites, like EUCATASTROPHE and EUSTRESS.

It may be seldom used, but it is nevertheless good to know that a word as fundamentally positive as *respair* exists, especially in difficult and challenging times. And knowing that it takes the merest of changes – just replacing one letter, in fact – to turn our hopelessness around, perhaps makes it all the more comforting a concept.

See also: dolorifuge

SELF-SOOTHE

≋

for when you're having trouble sleeping

When we have a lot on our mind, one of the first casualties of our addled brain is a decent night's sleep. Mulling over our worries and troubles becomes such an obsession that we find it difficult to switch off our thoughts even late at night, and before long – no matter how physically exhausted we might feel – we find ourselves lying awake in bed, worrying and stressing over everything we can possibly think of. If we're finally able to get any sleep, we wake the next day feeling utterly *rammist* – a word colourfully defined by a dictionary of 1838 as 'half-asleep, half-awake', and suffering from a 'conglomerated state of one's ideas, which continues for some time after being prematurely awakened from sleep'.

Sleeplessness is often a self-worsening cycle too. After all, no sleep-deprived brain is ever going to come

up with a sensible, well-thought-out solution to all
our problems – and if it's our problems that are keeping us awake at night, then that cycle is only going to
continue.

Being kept awake by our concerns or worries into
the early hours of the morning is so universal a problem
that a word for precisely this problem is among one
of the earliest recorded words in the English language.
'The Wife's Lament', or 'The Woman's Complaint' as
it is also known, is a poem included in *The Exeter Book*,
an anthology of Old English poetry and verse written
sometime in the late tenth century. Although countless
conflicting interpretations of 'The Wife's Lament' have
been proposed over the years, the poem essentially opens
with a woman mourning the absence of her husband,
who has left her and their family and headed out to sea.
Ever since then, she laments, she has suffered endlessly
from loneliness, despair and *uhtcearu* – an ancient Old
English word essentially meaning 'dawn-worries'. Put
another way, the woman has found herself struggling
to sleep, while she frets about the whereabouts of her
husband.

Despite its obvious usefulness, the word *uhtcearu* did
not catch on in Old English, and so no direct descendant
of it exists in the language today. In its place, we have

to make do with a handful of other words to do with wakefulness, restlessness and insomnia.

Inquiescentialness, for instance, is a seventeenth-century word for the lack of the peace and quiet needed to fall asleep. *Matutolypea* is a word for a feeling of grumpiness or downheartedness experienced first thing in the morning. Derived from *Matuta*, the name of a little-known Roman goddess of the morning, it is essentially the grown-up, classically educated version of 'getting out of the wrong side of the bed'. To *vigilate* is to lie awake at night unable to sleep. Unsurprisingly, it is related to the word *vigil*, which literally means 'awake' in Latin, and was originally adopted into English to refer to an unresting period of nocturnal religious devotion, observed on the eve of a holy day. If you're *wakerife*, or *waukrife*, then you're literally 'rife' with wakefulness, or disinclined to sleep. Perhaps as a consequence, *wakerife* can also be used as a noun to mean 'someone who is capable of making do with only a few hours' rest'. One word the English language could well do with adopting is the Irish *iarmhaireacht* – a feeling of lonesomeness or solitude that seems especially worse in the early hours of the morning, or, as one 1904 *Irish–English Dictionary* puts it, 'loneliness felt at cock-crow'.

Happily, there is just as rich a vocabulary of words to see us off to sleep as there are words to describe our lack of it. *Ataraxy*, for instance, is absolute calmness or piece of mind. *Easedom* is total comfort and freedom from stress or anxiety. To be *unsoulclogged* is to be literally 'not weighed down in spirit', while *euthymy* is perfect tranquillity and security. Both *cataphor* (derived from a Greek word meaning 'to bring down') and *subeth* (a medical term, derived from the Arabic for 'lethargy') are age-old terms for a deep and utterly undisturbed sleep. The *concubium* is the dead of night, or the period of your soundest, most peaceful sleep. And in nineteenth-century slang, an *admiral's watch* was a good night's rest, or else a prime opportunity to catch up on missed sleep. Quite why such an opportunity would be specifically associated with an admiral is unclear, but the term itself nevertheless referred originally to a change in or redistribution of the normal order of the ship's watches, which could have the effect of providing a crew member a one-off, longer-than-normal break from his duties.

If all that we're after is a good night's sleep, then perhaps the only word we really need in our lives is *self-soothe*. Dating back to the sixteenth century in English, *self-soothing* originally referred to the act of calming, flattering or even deluding oneself. But sparked by early childcare manuals compiled in the nineteenth century, *self-soothe* eventually came to be used to mean 'to be able to send yourself peacefully back off to sleep'. And what more could anyone ask for than that?

See also: frowst, hurkle-durkle

STOUND

~

for when you're grieving

Grief is one of the hardest, most painful and most challenging human emotions to endure. No matter whose loss we are mourning, the bitterest truth of grief is that the only thing that could ever possibly dispel it – seeing and talking to our lost loved one once more – is the one thing that simply cannot happen. Its only cure is an absolute impossibility.

If the person that we have lost is also the one person to whom we would have turned in times as difficult or as challenging as dealing with a loss, then our grief is even more difficult to bear.

The shock and pain of losing someone does eventually fade, as that initial grief steadily turns into the longer process of grieving. Words like MINDING and MONTH'S-MIND might help with that process, but it is still one that takes time. Indeed, it may take many weeks and months for our lives to adjust to whatever the new normal might now be, and for us slowly to begin to return to our usual selves as we learn to live with (or rather, or in spite of) the loss we have endured.

Our grief might fade in this period of recovery, but it never goes away. There is a word that is well worth knowing in such circumstances.

Stound is an ancient and largely forgotten word that first emerged in the Old English period as *stund* – a general word used of a brief moment, or any short period of time. To do something *stoundmeal* once meant to do it gradually or bit by bit, while something that occurs *umbestound* occurs only sometimes or occasionally, or at regular intervals. By extension, *stound* also came to be used of anything that lasted only a short time, a momentary thought or notion, a short, shooting pain or twinge, or a momentary thrill of excitement or delight.

None of these words or senses survived in standard English much after the fifteenth and sixteenth centuries. But a handful survived in isolation in a number of regional dialects, where their modern descendants endured long enough to be recorded in regional dictionaries and glossaries as recently as the early 1900s.

Based on its earlier meaning of a short twinge or momentary pain, in some Scots and northern English dialects the word *stound* came to be used of a sudden pang of grief and sadness when a loss – at the time, no longer at the forefront of our mind – is suddenly remembered. This will be a feeling familiar to anyone who has ever endured a loss: as time moves on and the initial pain diminishes, grief can be sparked back into action, often provoked by only the least likely or most superficial of things.

Knowing that there is a word for this sudden and painful pang of grief is comforting in itself. Knowing that the word has been in use in this context since the nineteenth century is heartening, as it proves that this painfulness is nothing new. Knowing that someone else – at some place and some time in history – thought this phenomenon meaningful enough to warrant its own word proves perhaps the most comforting fact of all: in grief, we are by no means alone.

See also: minding, month's-mind

STRAVAIG

≈

for when you're feeling confused or muddle-headed

Having too many tasks at once, or feeling as if your mind is racing with too many ideas or errands to deal with can be overwhelming and disorienting. It's hardly a unique feeling. The dictionary has a whole vocabulary of different words for muddled-headedness and confusion, ranging from the likes of *conglumrified* ('stupefied with a mixture of very foolish thoughts', according to one 1824 definition) to *hulver-headed* (a nineteenth-century invention, literally 'having a head like a holly-bush').

Calming, reorganising and otherwise sorting out your thoughts is imperative when your mind is racing and your to-do list is overflowing with unfinished jobs. But arguably one of the best ways of clearing your mind and calming your thoughts is even simpler than that: a walk in the fresh air.

To walk around on foot is to *peripateticate* – or at least it was according to the then Poet Laureate Robert Southey, who coined that particular word in the late eighteenth century. Southey based his invention on the earlier adjective *peripatetic*, which has since come to be used of occupations (and in particular teaching positions) that involve working in different locations. The missing link between these two meanings is *Peripatetic*-with-a-capital-P, which has long been used as a word for a follower or advocate of the Ancient Greek philosopher Aristotle.

Aristotle reportedly had a habit of taking a leisurely stroll through the halls, corridors and gardens of the Lyceum while he instructed and debated with students, and this meandering behaviour earned him and his fol- lowers the nickname *Peripatetikos*. Etymologically, that nickname brings together the Greek words *peri*, mean- ing 'around' or 'about' (as in *perimeter* and *periphery*), and *pateo*, meaning 'to walk' or 'tread' (which is a distant relative of the English word *path*). So *Peripatetikos*, and by extension *peripatetic*, essentially means 'given to walk- ing about'.

When *Peripatetic* first appeared in English in the fifteenth century, the word still referred exclusively to Aristotelian advocates, beliefs and techniques. But having an understanding of its etymology (and, no doubt, of Aristotle's habit for wandering around), later writers eventually commandeered the word *peripatetic* and began to apply it in several more literal senses, to variously mean 'a person who wanders', 'an itinerant pedlar' and, ultimately, 'someone who works in various locations'. It finally fell to Southey to invent the derivative *peripateticate* in 1793.

Other equally wonderful words for idly wandering and strolling around include *galivandering*, *trammocking*, *measening* and *horbgorbling*. Virginia Woolf preferred her own word *vagulate*, meaning 'to wander around in a vague manner'. To *noctivagate* is to wander at night, while a *nightraker* is someone who likes to do precisely that. If you're *solivagant*, then you prefer to walk alone. If you're *montivagant*, then you like to walk around the mountains. And if you're *mundivagant*, then the world is your oyster: you like to wander around the world.

It might not quite be feasible for you to stroll around the entire globe to help clear your mind, in which case why not just settle for *stravaiging*?

A word first recorded in the eighteenth century, *stravaig* is probably an aphetic (a linguistically beheaded) form of the word *extravage* – which is itself an alternative form of another word on this list, EXTRAVAGATE. When it first appeared in the eighteenth century, *stravaiging* was probably intended to have a more specific meaning, akin to 'hiking' or 'rambling'. As it became more widely used, across a patchwork of dialects throughout Scotland, Ireland and northern England, *stravaig* began to be used more loosely. Before long, it had simply come to mean 'to wander', particularly in an aimless, idling or casual manner – frankly, the perfect kind of walk for clearing your mind and granting yourself some much needed time to think.

See also: catacosmesis, cultellation, villeggiatura

SYMMACHY

≈

for when you see someone struggle

While we're busy focusing on words to help us with our own problems here, it's worth remembering that sometimes it can be just as troubling to see those around us, whom we care about and are close to, coping with their own challenges and unkind times. Whether they're dealing with relationship struggles, health issues or any of the other difficulties that fill these pages, seeing somebody close to us be compelled to meet a challenge can be hugely distressing.

It is in times such as these that we need to remember (and those around us need to know) that these fights need not be fought alone. One word for precisely that is *colluctation*.

Derived from a Latin word *luctare*, meaning 'to fight' or 'to wrestle', when it first appeared in the language in the 1600s, *colluctation* was used simply to describe any instance of contention or strife. But hidden in its etymology is an important detail: that initial *col-* is a form of the prefix *com-*, widely used to create words bearing some sense of doing, forming, working or enduring something together. So just as we have words such as *collide* ('a striking together'), *colleague* ('a co-worker') and *colloquium* ('a talking together'), we also have *collachrymation* ('the act of weeping together'), *collugency* ('a mutual mourning together') and *collucent* ('describing two or more things that are alight or ablaze together'). A *colluctation* is a 'fighting together'.

The problem with that definition is that it can be interpreted in two ways. In a positive sense, a 'fighting together' could imply two or more people joining forces to help one another through some troublesome patch. But this relatively simple meaning could also be interpreted in a more negative sense, referring to two or more people with a mutual difference, battling against each other in some bitter wrangle or conflict. And indeed over the centuries that it has been in (albeit fairly infrequent) use in the language, *colluctation* has been applied in both these collaborative and combative senses.

Perhaps what we need here, then, is a word that refers exclusively to the former – and, luckily, we have it.

Symmachy is another word from seventeenth-century English. Built from two Greek roots – *syn*, meaning 'together', and *makhe*, meaning 'battle' or 'fight' – it referred originally to a wartime or military alliance, forged by disparate parties united by a need to overcome some mutual adversary. 'A joining together in war against a common enemy', as one 1658 dictionary eloquently put it.

In a looser sense, however, *symmachy* merely describes aid, cooperation or the joining together of allied forces against something. Whenever we see anyone we care about facing a challenge, *symmachy* is there to remind us to give them all the help and support they need. Quite what form that support takes is irrelevant: it could be nothing more than a much needed hug or a sympathetic ear, or something more substantial, like your time, or your best advice and good counsel. No matter the situation, just being there in *symmachy*, to support those around us when we need them, is an important and effective gift.

See also: traumatropism, zivilcourage

TERTIUM COMPARATIONIS

≈

for when you're dealing with disunion

No matter what side of the political coin you happen to find yourself on, there's little denying that in recent years we have become part of a much more embittered, splintered and fractious world. Issue after contentious issue has forced its way into the forefront of the public mind, and a potent cocktail of 24-hour news cycles, unregulated social media, provocative punditry and elements of a news media motivated by whipping up metaphorical storms has ended up amplifying and entrenching opinions on all sides of all arguments.

Quite how or when (or indeed if) this ever more deep-seated disunion will heal itself is anyone's guess. But in these increasingly divided times, happily, there are a number of words and phrases that are well worth holding on to.

We've already looked here at *colluctation* and SYM-MACHY, a pair of words built around fighting together for a common cause. We can add to that *mutuality*, a sixteenth-century word for fellow feeling or shared experiences. *Omnibenevolence* is unendingly widespread kindness, to all people and things. *Sympolity* is cooperation and coordination between the citizens of a town or country.

In nineteenth-century naval slang, *remember your next astern* was a proverbial warning to treat others only as you would wish them to treat you. Supposedly derived from the text of a warning sign often displayed in the bridges of vast naval steamers, its words allude to the need for every ship in a fleet sailing together 'in column' (in a grid-like formation) to follow a true course, and thereby maintain a safe distance from one another. One ship sailing erratically or following a faltering course could disrupt the entire formation, as other ships jostled to maintain their position.

In a similarly cooperative fashion, *sympneumatism* is a bizarre word for an equally bizarre nineteenth-century belief that all human beings are somehow connected on an invisible, spiritual level. The term is credited to a South African-born diplomat, adventurer and Christian mystic (and one-time Member of Parliament for Stirling) named Laurence Oliphant, who published a guide to his theory of *Sympneumata; or, Evolutionary Forces Now Active in Man* in 1885. Oliphant's philosophy was based around the existence of 'spiritual spouses', or *sympneumata* (derived from *pneuma*, a Greek word for the soul, or a breath of life), and the handbook he published on his theory was, he claimed, at least partly dictated to him via clairvoyant connection to his late wife, Alice. 'One closes the book, not altogether certain of his meaning,' wrote a bemused Aldous Huxley in 1936. Perhaps for good reason, Oliphant's idea of *sympneumatism* has long since been abandoned – although the word itself remains a useful term for any seemingly invisible connection between all human beings.

Leaving questionable Victorian pseudoscience to one side, there is a better term for remembering that all of us have much more in common than that which divides us: *tertium comparationis* is a Latin expression that literally means 'the third part of the comparison'.

Originally a term from rhetoric and logic, *tertium comparationis* is essentially the missing link between two things that are being metaphorically or somehow figuratively compared. In the sentence, 'He is just as successful as her', the missing link between the man and woman being compared – the *tertium comparationis* – is success.

Often the writer or creator of a comparison of this kind is not (or rather, does not need to be) quite so explicit in directing their audience to the identity of this unmentioned third element. Instead, they leave it up to the intuition and imagination of the audience to work out their intended meaning from their knowledge of the two things being compared. Imagine, for instance, that a person walks into an especially cold room, and exclaims, 'It's like an igloo in here!' By not explicitly mentioning the temperature, the speaker ultimately leaves it up to the audience to work out from their knowledge of the two elements in question (igloos and the room they are both in) precisely what it is the speaker means. Factors that do not apply (presumably the hearer will successfully infer that the speaker is not commenting on the room being built from snow and ice, or lacking any windows, or being hemispherical in shape) are mentally jettisoned, until the most likely *tertium comparationis* (in this case the relative coldness of the room) remains. If the metaphor is meaningful, then anyone hearing or reading it should have no problem in instantly figuring out what is being inferred.

Although strictly a rhetorical term, just like Laurence Oliphant's dubious theory of *sympneumatism*, we can interpret *tertium comparationis* as a broader reminder that often, beneath the surface of two seemingly unrelated things, there is still much that connects us. People divided by different political views, for instance, regardless of how irreconcilable they might appear, are still – we trust – driven by an overall desire to improve the world around us; it is just that the holders of these views have different goals, and different methods of achieving them. It is only the common ground between these two extremes – the *tertium comparationis* – that stands any hope of healing and uniting them, representing as it does a point where differing parties can meet and agree, and from there work together to figure out a shared solution to their problems. In these divided and disunited times, this obscure term from ancient rhetoric could well prove an expression worth holding on to in the twenty-first century.

TRAUMATROPISM

≈

for when you're worried about the environment

Perhaps one of the saddest words added to our language in recent times is *solastalgia*, a neologism coined by the Australian academic Glenn Albrecht as recently as 2005. As both an environmentalist and a philosopher, Albrecht studies the connections between human health and the health of the environment around us, and how problems in the wider environment can have a detrimental effect both on our physical and mental health – disorders he classes as *somaterratic* and *psychoterratic*. Of these two categories, *solastalgia* falls into the second: it describes mental anguish or distress that is the direct result of climate change.

In introducing the term in 2005, Albrecht drew parallels between *solastalgia* and *nostalgia*, which likewise derives from a Greek word meaning 'pain', *algos*.

But while *nostalgia* essentially refers to homesickness, or a longing for home when far away from familiar surroundings, *solastalgia* affects those whose home has changed around them, leaving them mourning for a place that no longer resembles what it once did, or that simply no longer exists.

'Solastalgia is not about looking back to some golden past, nor is it about seeking another place as "home",' he wrote. Instead, it is 'a form of homesickness one gets when one is still at home'.

Just as nostalgia was once considered a genuine medical condition (see HEAFGANG), so too is the medical world coming round to the notion of *solastalgia*, highlighting just how pressing the fight to salvage our climate and environment is becoming, and how powerless many people feel in response to it. In 2015, *The Lancet* included the term in a landmark paper on the interaction between human and environmental health, and in 2017 the American Psychological Association officially added a similar term, *ecoanxiety* – defined as 'chronic fear of environmental doom' – to its official list of diagnoses.

We can all do our utmost to improve (or, at least, not to exacerbate) the situation, but climate change is an existential problem that will require many years of action and cooperation, across borders and generations, to solve. Whether a solution of that magnitude can ever be enacted in time remains to be seen.

The strength and resilience of nature, however, is remarkable, and there is a word worth holding on to that might give us hope. Coined in the nineteenth century, *traumatropism* refers to the misshapen regrowth of a plant or tree as a result of earlier damage or trauma. A tree that has been struck by lightning or stunted by fire, for instance, might end up growing in some wildly misshapen direction as a result of the injury. A tree part-felled by gales might continue to grow, despite now leaning at some outrageous angle in the midst of its forest. And a plant pruned too harshly might yet survive, given enough time – albeit now beaten back into some unlikely and unusual shape.

Traumatropism, and countless similar examples, remind us is that nature is more robust than we could ever imagine. From forest fires to flash floods, the problems and hardships nature faces are extreme, but the world around us is hardy and – though it might not return in the same way as before – nature always manages to win many more battles than it loses. In the years to come, we have to hope that it proves hardy enough to overcome the damage we have caused it.

See also: aphercotropism, meliorism, symmachy

VILLEGGIATURA

≈

for when you're feeling
city-weary

The hustle and bustle of life in a city can be energising and inspiring. Cities offer practically everything you could possibly want, whenever you could possibly want it. And with a near perpetual throng of people and a vast network of unfamiliar streets, cities present the constant possibility of stumbling across someone or somewhere new that will open up and enrich your life even further.

Yet all that activity and commotion can prove wearying. Cities might have much more to offer compared with our smaller towns and villages, but that is not to say that quieter places have nothing to offer in return. Peacefulness, solitude, fresh air and a tighter, closer community are for many people all irresistible draws. The further we drift from urban areas into the wider woods and wilds, the more acute – and the more tantalising – all these factors become.

All of this is encapsulated in a number of wonderful words the dictionary has to offer celebrating our love of the great outdoors. Since the seventeenth century people have been *rusticating* – a verb meaning 'to visit the countryside', or, as the *Oxford English Dictionary* puts it, 'to live a quiet country life'. It's a lifestyle that you might particularly enjoy if you're *nemorivagant*, an equally ancient and long-forgotten word describing someone or something who likes to wander in the woods. And while it has yet to be adopted into English, it's worth bearing in mind too that the striking Japanese word *shinrin-yoku* means 'the act of taking a trip to the woods purely to improve your well-being'. Appropriately enough, it literally means 'forest-bathing'.

To *spaw* is 'to go to the seaside . . . for a pleasure trip', according to the *English Dialect Dictionary*, while a *spawing-spot* was a seaside resort in nineteenth-century English; both words are probably derived from nothing more than a local corruption of 'spa'. And while you're at the coast, you might like to take a *scud* – an old Scots word for a journey on a sailing boat, taken purely for pleasure (which somewhat alarmingly derives from an even earlier word for the skimming of a stone across the surface of water).

Of all the words worth bearing in mind here, however, perhaps one of the best is an Italian loanword first adopted into English in the mid eighteenth century. A *villeggiatura* is a trip or vacation to a country retreat, and in particular one enjoyed as a break from the busyness of everyday life, or as a means of restoring your health and well-being.

Villeggiatura derives simply from the Italian *villa*, which as a word for a grand country residence – and in particular one in its own grounds, or attached to a working farm or estate – probably has its roots in the Latin word for a village, *vicus*. *Villa* itself was borrowed into English in the early 1600s, with *villeggiatura* emerging a little over a century later at the height of popularity for the European Grand Tour – the continent-spanning, culturally and educationally inspiring excursion undertaken by wealthy young men when they had come of age in the seventeenth and eighteenth centuries.

The days of the Grand Tour might long since have passed, but restorative, inspiring trips into the countryside have never fallen out of fashion.

See also: stravaig

VIOLON D'INGRES

≋

for when you're work obsessed

Jean-Auguste-Dominique Ingres was born in Montauban, in south-west France, in 1780. Aged just seventeen, he relocated to Paris to pursue his dream of becoming an artist, winning the Royal Academy's top prize in 1801 and exhibiting his first work at the renowned Paris Salon the following year. But that first flush of success quickly ended. Further critical acclaim proved harder to come by, and for the next two decades Ingres' work was met with only meagre praise among the harsh and discerning critics of the Paris art world. Finally, after a long period of study in Italy, Ingres finally achieved the recognition he deserved when his painting *The Vow of Louis XIII* (1824) was met with near universal acclaim. The work established him as the leading neo-classical artist of the time, earned him the job of director of the Paris Academy in Rome and secured him his place among France's most accomplished artists. Ingres, however, was not just a painter. In fact, in a literal sense, he had another string to his bow.

In childhood Ingres had studied the violin, and before relocating to Paris in 1797, had played second violin with an orchestra in Toulouse. Although he never pursued his violin playing professionally, as he did his skill as a painter, Ingres nonetheless never let his musical facility slide. While serving as Academy director in Rome, he often played the violin with the Academy's music students, and when the great pianist and composer Franz Liszt arrived in Italy in 1839, he and Ingres – who was called on to show Liszt the city's many sights – bonded over their mutual love of Beethoven. Together, they played a number of Beethoven's sonatas for piano and violin, and Liszt was impressed enough by Ingres' playing that he went on to dedicate two piano transcriptions of Beethoven symphonies to his newfound friend. In return, Ingres sketched a now famous portrait of the then twenty-eight-year-old composer.

As is often the case with artists, Ingres' reputation continued to flourish after his death in 1867, and it was only in the later 1800s and early 1900s that the extraordinary legacy he had left the art world began to be realised. But his dual interest in both music and painting led to another, slightly more unexpected legacy: the *violon d'Ingres*.

Literally meaning 'Ingres' violin', the expression *violon d'Ingres* is used to refer to any skill, pastime or other similar interest – separate from your main work, or the field in which you are best known – in which you also excel or are just as equally proficient. It was first recorded in a 1931 dictionary of French, which noted in its definition that a 'fairly suspect legend' claimed that Ingres had, throughout his life and career, always been more proud of his violin playing than of his painting, despite it being his painting that brought him his greatest success. That explanation might be overstepping the mark a little, but it nevertheless helped to establish Ingres' place in the language: the phrase had soon fallen into more widespread use in its native French, and by the 1960s had become sufficiently well known to be adopted into English. The *Oxford English Dictionary*'s earliest record of the term comes from a newspaper report referring to the US President Eisenhower's proficiency as a golfer.

It might be a century old (and the name behind it a century older than that), but there is much we can take from the *violon d'Ingres*. That doesn't mean that we need to be a secret virtuoso violinist or a closet concert pianist away from work; Ingres' violin playing might have been proficient enough to have impressed Franz Liszt, but what concerns us more here is the fact that he pursued it and enjoyed it.

The *violon d'Ingres* is a word for anyone who finds themselves too wholly absorbed in their work, or whose day-to-day routine leaves them little to no time for themselves. It is a word that stresses the importance of taking our mind off our work or career every so often, escaping our usual workday bubble, and focusing instead on something we purely and simply enjoy doing. It is a word that reminds us of the motivating, calming, re-energising quality of doing precisely that.

See also: cultellation, gadwaddick

WORLDCRAFT

≈

for when you're worried about ageing

It comes to us all, of course, but growing old isn't always the most welcome or easy to accept of life's experiences. With our advancing years come challenges – both physical and mental – and as each year passes these challenges can become ever more unkind and difficult to ignore.

These difficulties are borne out in the language too. Search the dictionary and you'll come across countless words such as *owden* (an ancient Yorkshire dialect word, meaning 'to feel the effects of advancing years'), *eilden-cumbered* ('held back by age') and *braigle* ('someone or something rendered useless through age or overuse'). To *maun* is to tremble with weakness or infirmity. To be *dottered*, or *doitified*, is to be slowed or muddled in one's thinking, due to old age. And, derived from an old dialect name for a gnarled, aged or fallen tree, the tragically poignant word *runnel* means 'an aged person who has outlived all of their friends'. The worries and problems of old age are, it seems, profound and widespread.

One of the positives of our advancing age is the wisdom and life experience that it brings with it. As an old Swedish proverb evocatively puts it, *the afternoon knows what the morning never suspected*: that which would have shocked, disappointed, confounded or astounded us in our youth can ultimately be explained, expected, prepared for and buffered against in our advancing years, thanks to nothing more than the extensive knowledge we accrue merely by living our lives. Imparting that lifetime's worth of knowledge and understanding onto those younger than us can be one of the most rewarding aspects of growing old.

This is all neatly summed up in the seldom used (and arguably somewhat dramatic-sounding) word *worldcraft*.

Appropriately enough for a term we're tying in with our advancing years, *worldcraft* is a notably ancient term: its earliest record in the language comes from as far back as the late tenth century, in a letter penned by a prolific Anglo-Saxon writer and grammarian known as Ælfric of Eynsham. Back then, in early Old English, *worldcraft* meant literally what it says: works of art or craftsman-ship that were secular – of our world – as opposed to those that were divinely inspired, or completed for the glory of God or the Church. As the meaning of the word *craft* altered over time, the meaning of *worldcraft* altered with it.

Having long fallen by the linguistic wayside, by the time it reappeared in our language in the seventeenth century it had come to be used to refer to worldly wisdom – skills or knowledge of the world fostered over time merely through life experience. It is essentially the product of a lifetime of experiences and encounters, successes and failures, adventures, exploits and learning. There is no other way of accruing this *worldcraft* other than living a long life.

See also: beauté du diable, opsimathy

THE WORSE THE PASSAGE, THE MORE WELCOME THE PORT

≈

*for when you're struggling
or losing hope*

Every word in this collection is about being kind to ourselves and others, curing and calming our worries and problems, restoring hope and maintaining positivity.

We all suffer through difficult periods in our lives, and often all that we can hope is that they don't endure, and that we have the strength in ourselves and in those around us to see them through. But while many of the words and phrases included here are attached to individual problems and troublesome feelings, how about something to bear in mind when you are just generally struggling to remain focused or hopeful?

We could, in these situations, return to a word such as the glorious EUCATASTROPHE. Or we could turn to some equally fortuitous word, like a *say-shot* (an eighteenth-century term for an unexpected chance to restore everything that has been lost), or a *sloven's-year* (a period of unexpected good fortune or bounty – a year so fruitful that even the most slovenly of farmers can harvest a decent crop). But while those words can help to dispel our most pessimistic thoughts and tendencies, relying on some whimsical future change of fate to improve our lot and solve the problems we face now is, in reality, fairly imprudent. There is certainly an outside chance that difficult circumstances might change of their own accord, but it is far more likely that we might simply need to weather the storm and see off our challenges ourselves as best we can. For that, we can take heart in a long-forgotten eighteenth-century proverb.

In 1732, an English physician and clergyman named Thomas Fuller published the *Gnomologia*, a collection of what he described as 'adages and proverbs, wise sentences and witty sayings'. The work includes some of the earliest records of such wise words as *great oaks from little acorns grow* and *the early bird catches the worm*, as well as more than six thousand less-well-known (but no less astute) sayings from the time like *hunger is the best sauce, a light purse makes a heavy heart* and *a crowd is not a company*. And number 4,848 in Fuller's immense catalogue is the saying, *the worse the passage, the more welcome the port*.

How popular or well established this expression was in the language by the time Fuller included it in his *Gnomologia* is unclear; the fact that there is no written record of it for another six decades suggests it was never particularly well known. But in 1792, the English clergyman and evangelist John Burridge not only reused Fuller's phrase but elaborated on it further in a letter written to 'a Christian friend' who was currently enduring what Burridge labelled 'sore trouble'. In a footnote to his letter, Burridge emphasised his belief that the more acute his friend's suffering is now, the more he will ultimately be rewarded for having endured it in the future. 'The more obstinate the contest, the more glorious the victory,' he wrote. 'The more dangerous the voyage, the more welcome the port. The heavier the cross, the brighter the crown.'

Admittedly, any one of Burridge's three versions of this old adage could serve us well here, but it is Fuller's earlier phrase, *the worse the passage, the more welcome the port*, that seems the most apt. Despite its simplicity, it implies two worthwhile truths that it would benefit us to remember when enduring any kind of hardship. For one, it reminds us that nearly all hardships eventually come to an end. No matter what we might currently be enduring – and no matter how unlikely or remote an end to our troubles may seem – just as a storm-tossed ship eventually finds its way back to port, our problems are likely to diminish eventually. Secondly, it implies that the harsher and more arduous our troubles are at the moment, when they do finally resolve themselves and allow us to return to our normal lives, we will be stronger, wiser and all the more relieved for having endured them. Even in our harshest experiences there is always much to be learned.

See also: eucatastrophe, meliorism

XENODOCHY

≈

for when you're confronting xenophobia

In these divided times, it can often seem as if society has become less welcoming and less collaborative, and is instead ever more hostile, intolerant and suspicious.

The word *xenophobia* has emerged as something of a watchword for these difficult times. For what seems like such an arcane word, *xenophobia* is in fact not much more than a century old, having been coined as relatively recently as 1880 in an article in the *London Daily News*. Before then, English had made do with the considerably older word *misoxeny*, derived from the same root as words such as *misanthropy* and *misogyny*, which date back to the early 1600s.

All the phobias in the English language trace back, via Latin, to the Ancient Greek word for 'fear', *phobos*. Attached to it here is the Greek word *xenos*, meaning 'stranger' or 'foreigner' – making a *xenophobe* someone who fears or exhibits a hatred of outsiders.

Xenophobia is a demoralising word, which smacks of closed borders, closed minds and a failure to communicate, collaborate and understand those who happen to have been born on the other side of the lines we draw on maps. Oddly, however, a wonderful antidote to the poison of *xenophobia* lies just a few words away on the same page of the dictionary.

One of the great ironies of the word *xenophobia* – and, perhaps, one of the lessons we could learn about how outsiders were treated in Ancient Greece – is that the Greek word for 'stranger', *xenos*, could also be used to mean 'house guest', 'refugee', 'visitor' or, more vaguely, 'someone requesting or deserving of hospitality'. Based on those readings of the word, English has amassed a vast and often overlooked vocabulary of tolerance and open-mindedness towards strangers that is just waiting to be tapped into. A *xenodochium*, for instance, is a guesthouse, or a house or room in which strangers or visitors are made welcome. *Philoxeny*, the long-lost opposite of *misoxeny*, is a term from the early 1600s for a love of hospitality, or of welcoming strangers to your home (while *philoxenist* is someone who does precisely that). A *xenial* relationship is an especially friendly or compassionate one between a guest and their host. A *xenogogue* is someone who helps or directs strangers; travel guides in sixteenth-century English were like-wise sometimes titled *xenogogies*. And amid all of these 'x' words is *xenodochy*, described by one seventeenth-century dictionary as another word for hospitality, or the entertainment of strangers.

In this way, *xenodochy* is in many ways the polar opposite of *xenophobia*. Whereas *xenophobia* seeks to reinforce differences and contrasts, *xenodochy* seeks to find a common ground. Here, doors and borders are not closed, but thrown open. Strangers are not shunned or met with hostility, but welcomed warmly, and met with unending hospitality. *Xenodochy* is a word of tolerance and empathy, curiosity and cooperation. And if ever a new watchword for our modern world were needed, this is surely it.

ZENOBIA

≋

for when you're suffering from impostor syndrome

In psychiatry, *impostor syndrome* is the phenomenon whereby a person so doubts their own abilities that, even when presented with evidence of their own achievements, they convince themselves that they're not worthy of success and will surely some day be found to be a talentless fraud – or, for want of a better word, an 'impostor'.

In some instances, certain high-achieving people *do* turn out to be somewhat ill suited to their lofty positions, but this is by no means a word for any of them. Those suffering impostor syndrome genuinely are talented and deserving of all their success, but sadly convince themselves otherwise.

Also known merely as *impostorism*, the term *impostor syndrome* was first used in a 1978 study by US psychologists

Pauline Clance and Suzanne Imes. Over five years, they conducted a series of in-depth interviews with more than 150 highly successful, high-achieving women, but found that despite their 'earned degrees, scholastic honours, high achievement on standardised tests, praise and professional recognition from colleagues and respected authorities', many of the women felt no sense of success. In fact, far from it: instead, many of them wrote off their professional and academic successes to good fortune, oversights in the employment-selection process, or to being overvalued or held in too high a regard by their colleagues. They felt that they were merely 'impostors', who had fooled all those around them into thinking that they were intelligent or deserving of success. And, as the authors of the study described it, the interviews uncovered countless examples of this 'individual experience of self-perceived intellectual phoniness'.

Subsequent studies have drawn parallels between *impostor syndrome* and several other psychiatric phenomenon. So-called *self-handicapping*, for instance, describes an instance of self-sabotage in which a person deliberately hampers their own efforts in an attempt to pre-explain their own failure. The *Jonah complex* (see TO PIPE IN AN IVY LEAF) accounts for why someone might fail to achieve their full potential out of the fear of facing new challenges and situations. And the *Horner effect* is a theory intended to demonstrate how women in particular are almost preconditioned to fear – and ultimately shy away from – success. Named after its pioneer, the American psychologist Matina Horner, the *Horner effect* was the result of a 1970 psychological study in which a group of male college students were asked to complete a story with the opening line, 'John finds himself at the top of his medical school class', and a group of female students were asked to complete a story beginning, 'Anne finds herself at the top of her medical school class'. Despite the students being given entirely free rein in creating their stories, Anne was found to consistently appear in more negative tales than John, whose stories by comparison tended to end in more positive, prosperous endings. The female storytellers, the study suggested, were somehow preconditioned not to fear or worry about failure, but to fear being successful.

The problems that lie behind impostor syndrome and many of these similar phenomena are simultaneously wide-ranging – driven by broad, longstanding gender imbalances in society as a whole – and individual – driven by personal feelings of inadequacy or a lack of confidence. The solutions to these problems are just as complex, and far outside what any choice word plucked from the dictionary could ever hope to achieve. But there is one word – or rather, one name – the story behind which acts as an inspiring antidote here.

Zenobia was the name of a third-century queen of ancient Palmyra. Although the city today stands in ruins, in what is now modern-day Syria, in Zenobia's time Palmyra was a grand metropolis, and a province of the eastern Roman Empire. Her husband, Odaenathus, was the founder king of the so-called Palmyrene Kingdom, and via a series of successful battles and conflicts in the mid 200s essentially gained control of a Roman splinter state, occupying an impressive stretch of the Middle East between the Red, Black and Mediterranean Seas.

All of that, however, came to an abrupt end in 267 CE, when Odaenathus was assassinated along with his first-born son and heir, Hairan. Next in line to the throne was the couple's second son, Vaballathus, but he was just ten years old at the time, and so unable to rule effectively. Faced with a vacuum of power that threatened to precipitate the collapse of the entire kingdom, it fell to Zenobia to take *de facto* control of Palmyra. And she soon proved a more capable leader than anyone could have anticipated.

Over the years that followed, Zenobia greatly extended the reach of her kingdom, further advancing its borders into Arabia and Asia Minor, taking control of Egypt and the northern Nile corridor, and upgrading the Palmyrene Kingdom into a vast Palmyrene Empire. Educated, intelligent and benevolent, she made her court a seat of learning, and willingly accommodated all the different faiths and cultures of those who came under her influence. As empress, she routinely stood up to the threatening might of Rome, and in 271 CE took advantage of crises in the western flank of the Roman Empire to proclaim Palmyra independent of the embattled Roman Emperor Aurelian. At its peak, Zenobia's new Palmyrene Empire stretched from Ankara in the north to modern-day Aswan in Egypt, and on to Medina, on the coast of Saudi Arabia, in the south.

Zenobia's extraordinary reign was not to last. In 272, Aurelian's Roman army headed east, and defeated Zenobia's forces at the Battle of Immae, near Antioch, in southern Turkey. As a result, Palmyra was besieged, and both Zenobia and Vaballathus, who was still only fifteen years old, were captured before they could escape. Their fates are unknown (and much debated), but in their absence Palmyra eventually fell, and by 273 was once more under Roman control.

Zenobia's place in history was nevertheless assured. She had taken control of a vast kingdom at a critical point in its history (at a time when it was all but unheard of for a woman to wield such power) and had not only proved herself to be an incredibly courageous, ambitious and effective leader, but succeeded in extending her empire's range and influence to the greatest extent in its history. Hers is an astonishing story – and, moreover, it is one that lives on in the language to this day. Zenobia's name – a Greek invention, meaning 'derived of Zeus' – has since been adopted into the English language as an allusive term for any similarly powerful, courageous and unstoppably determined woman.

ZIVILCOURAGE

≋

*for when you witness wrongdoing
or fail to take action*

How many of us can say that, at some time in our lives, we have seen some unacceptable or upsetting situation, or have seen someone in trouble or witnessed something shocking or upsetting taking place, and to our shame have remained merely a passive bystander – or even worse, have simply walked away? Stepping into the fray when we see others bullied, disparaged, attacked or taken advantage of takes a considerable amount of bravery, not least because it so often comes at considerable risk to ourselves. But no matter what it is that we are witnessing, by involving ourselves and confronting the perpetrators – no matter who or what they might be – we are not only defending the defenceless, but defending the ethics and standards that we believe to be right in our society. From stepping in to break up an argument in the street to whistleblowing against the actions of some giant corporation, these individual acts of extraordinary bravery hold wrongdoers to account, regardless of their size and power, and irrespective of the risk involved.

In psychological terms, this bravery is known as *civil courage* – or, more often than not, by its adopted German name, *zivilcourage*. Behavioural psychologists have long debated how this courage differs from other similar forms of courageousness, heroism and altruism, and what variables can affect how likely a person is to step in to help. What sets *zivilcourage* aside, essentially, is that the courageous person who comes forward to help does so at great risk to themselves – and, more-over, they often do so instinctively, without considering the risk involved before acting. Put simply, *zivilcourage* is the courage to stand up for what you believe to be right, regardless of what the repercussions to you and your life might be.

In a world where angry division seems the order of the day – while community spiritedness becomes ever more difficult to come by – it is comforting to know that a word like *zivilcourage* exists. Surely this is a word not only to take heart from, but to take inspiration from;

the more we stand up for what we believe to be right, the more those who do not believe in the same rights, values and integrities are held to account.

See also: symmachy

ACKNOWLEDGEMENTS

Endless thanks as always to my exceptional agent, Andrew Lownie, and to the best publishing team I could hope for: Jennie Condell, Pippa Crane, Sarah Rigby, Marianne Thorndahl, Alison Menzies, and all at Elliott & Thompson.

Thanks to the wonderful Julie Nathanson for bringing an interfulgent light to my attention, and for being so encouraging and endlessly supportive.

Thanks to Mark Findlay, Pete Tuddenham and Oliver James for keeping me sane at seven o'clock in the morning, and to Chris Kirk for encouraging me, this book and everything else back on the right track.

Katie Watson – in a book about words, ironically there are not enough to thank you for your help, advice, time, kindness and cups of coffee over the past twelve months. I don't think this book or this author would quite be here without you.

Mam and Dad. Love and miss you forever.

ABOUT THE AUTHOR

PAUL ANTHONY JONES is the author of several books on trivia and language, including *Around the World in 80 Words*, *The Cabinet of Linguistic Curiosities*, *The Accidental Dictionary* and *Word Drops*. He appears regularly in the *Telegraph* online, BBC Radio 4's *World at One*, *Buzzfeed*, *Huffington Post* and *Mental Floss*, and has contributed to the *Guardian*, *Independent* and Oxford and Cambridge dictionaries online. He also runs @HaggardHawks, the hugely popular language-based Twitter account and YouTube channel. He lives in Newcastle upon Tyne.